ASIAN AMERICA
A series edited by Gordon H. Chang

The increasing size and diversity of the Asian American population, its growing significance in American society and culture, and the expanded appreciation, both popular and scholarly, of the importance of Asian Americans in the country's present and past—all these developments have converged to stimulate wide interest in scholarly work on topics related to the Asian American experience. The general recognition of the pivotal role that race and ethnicity have played in American life, and in relations between the United States and other countries, has also fostered this heightened attention.

Although Asian Americans were a subject of serious inquiry in the late nineteenth and early twentieth centuries, they were subsequently ignored by the mainstream scholarly community for several decades. In recent years, however, this neglect has ended, with an increasing number of writers examining a good many aspects of Asian American life and culture. Moreover, many students of American society are recognizing that the study of issues related to Asian America speak to, and may be essential for, many current discussions on the part of the informed public and various scholarly communities.

The Stanford series on Asian America seeks to address these interests. The series will include works from the humanities and social sciences, including history, anthropology, political science, American studies, law, literary criticism, sociology, and interdisciplinary and policy studies.

Consuming Citizenship

Consuming Citizenship

CHILDREN OF ASIAN IMMIGRANT
ENTREPRENEURS

Lisa Sun-Hee Park

STANFORD UNIVERSITY PRESS
STANFORD, CALIFORNIA

Stanford University Press
Stanford, California

Printed in the United States of America
on acid-free, archival-quality paper

Library of Congress Cataloging-in-Publication Data

Park, Lisa Sun-Hee.
    Consuming citizenship : children of Asian immigrant
entrepreneurs / Lisa Sun-Hee Park.
        p.   cm. — (Asian America)
    Includes bibliographical references and index.
    ISBN 0-8047-5247-8 (cloth : alk. paper)
    ISBN 0-8047-5248-6 (pbk. : alk. paper)
        1. Korean Americans—Cultural assimilation.   2. Chinese
Americans—Cultural assimilation.   3. Children of immigrants—
United States—Social conditions.   4. Immigrants—United
States—Social conditions.   5. Children of immigrants—United
States—Interviews.   6. Asian Americans—Interviews.   7. Family-
owned business enterprises—Social aspects—United States.
8. Consumption (Economics)—Social aspects—United States.
9. Korean Americans—Economic conditions.   10. Chinese
Americans—Economic conditions.   I. Title.   II.   Series.

E184.K6P365 2005
305.895 7073—DC22

                                                    2005013560

Original Printing 2005

Last figure below indicates year of this printing:
14   13   12   11   10   09   08   07

For My Sisters

Contents

Tables

Acknowledgments

I would like to thank all the young women and men who participated in this project. They were inspiring and their vivid stories will always stay with me. My thanks also to my fabulous research assistants: Christopher Sakai, Traci Brynne Voyles, Alex Urquhart, Bobby Hersberger, and Lorraine Saito.

Next, I would like to thank the chair of my dissertation committee at Northwestern University, Allan Schnaiberg. His unwavering support during this early stage was crucial and greatly appreciated. The other members of my committee, Gary Alan Fine and Albert Hunter, were instrumental as well. Also, my thanks to the American Sociological Association's Minority Fellows program and the Minority Opportunity Student Training Program for their funding support and for introducing me to a number of other amazing mentors whom I now consider friends, including David Takeuchi, Margaret Andersen, Carole Marks, and Morrison Wong.

Later, I had the opportunity to befriend and learn from a number of wonderful scholars and colleagues at the University of Colorado, Boulder. Here, I want to particularly thank Michiko Hase, Linda White, and Rachel Silvey for always bringing laughter into our work sessions. Thanks also to Kamala Kempadoo, Janet Jacobs, Joanne Belknap, and Anna Vayr in the Women Studies program for their support and assistance on this project. In Ethnic Studies, my other home at CU, I would like to thank Evelyn Hu-

DeHart, Lane Hirabayashi, and Jose Martinez for their comments and encouragement.

Next, I must acknowledge the many wonderful colleagues at the University of California, San Diego, particularly Jane Rhodes, a true friend since day one. In addition, I owe much to Lynn Hudson for her always incisive suggestions and hilarious observations. My thanks also to Yen Le Espiritu for her continued guidance and expertise. Denise Ferreira da Silva and Lisa E. Sanchez also provided key suggestions and encouragement.

I would also like to extend my gratitude to Carmen Borbón-Wu and the other editors at Stanford University Press for all their efforts in bringing this book to life. Their professionalism and dedication to this project made the process painless.

Finally, I would like to express my sincere gratitude to my family, especially my parents. Words cannot express how grateful I am for their kindness and love. And, to Jin-Young, a funny kid who keeps me going. Lastly, many, many, many thank-yous to David Naguib Pellow for everything and more.

L.S.P.

CHAPTER ONE

Consumptive Citizenship

> In July, my younger brother bought this little multimillion-dollar abode, in cash, for my parents. It goes well with the $100,000 black Mercedes S500 that will sit in the three-car garage. That was this year's Mother's Day present. Poor Pops only got a new computer. Growing up, we always knew how much our parents suffered for us so that we could live in golden America, land of the free. . . . My parents immigrated to a place where their professional degrees were not honored, and they had to take what were menial jobs in comparison. . . . [T]hey've always reminded us how much we owed them.
> —T. A. Lee, "A Good Son"[1]

This book critically examines the process by which Korean American and Chinese American children of entrepreneurial immigrants struggle to define themselves as *Americans*. In doing this, I strive to extend our understanding of immigrants and immigration beyond the usual premise of the immigrant narrative, which, at its core, is a story of upward mobility and individual integration into U.S. society. Embedded within this understanding of adaptation is an uncritical assumption of status attainment or upward economic mobility that necessitates the absorption of immigrants into a preexisting and unequal social hierarchy.[2] Whether in the earlier waves of immigration, as studied by Oscar Handlin, or in the current influx of newcomers, immigrants are repeatedly measured for "successful" adaptation.[3] All too often, studies of immigrant ethnic identity formation, work and labor, education attainment, and family, singularly focus on how well a particular immigrant group is absorbed into the United States.[4] This traditional framework leaves little room for critical assessments of the social hierarchy itself. Rather, it is the immigrant or children of immigrants, in this case, who are scrutinized for how well they negotiate the expectations of a new society. While this question may be appropriate and necessary in studying immigrants, it seems incomplete not to question the expectations as well. This critical absence is particularly egregious in studying children of immigrants who have grown up in the United States. I argue that for Asian *Americans*, the process in question is not whether or not they have adapted, but rather *why* Asian Americans are made to feel compelled to prove their "Americanness" and *how* Asian Americans display their social citizenship (or belonging).

My interviews with Korean and Chinese American children of immigrant entrepreneurs illustrate an underlying, consistent effort on their part to reassert their citizenship as legitimate within a contested political context that is, at best, ambivalent towards the growing presence of racially ethnic immigrants. What is evident is that these young adults have absorbed or "adapted" American culture quite readily; therefore, a more interesting question is *why* second generation Asian Americans feel compelled to remind others of their legitimate existence in the United States and *how* they go about exerting this citizenship status. The experiences of those raised in the setting of immigrant small family businesses are particularly enlightening in this regard given their embeddedness within a social institution that epitomizes the quintessential American ideology of success and upward mobility as exemplified by Horatio Alger's "rags to riches" stories.[5] Within this narrative of "Americanization," the primacy of conspicuous consumption of status symbols is evident in establishing their social rights as members of society. This study, then, examines the process by which Korean American and Chinese American children of entrepreneurial immigrants exert their social citizenship through consumption.

An analysis of the consumption of material goods is instructive in shedding light on how members of the Asian American second generation understand their position within a particular political and economic context.[6] For instance, in interview after interview with children of immigrant entrepreneurs, they brought up the issue of repaying obligations to their parents. Whether the discussion focused on immigration, their relationship with their parents, their work experience at the family store, or their future career goals, repayment for parental sacrifices was a central motivation for their own actions. This repayment was consistently expressed in consumptive terms. While some (mostly younger) respondents explicitly indicated the purchase of particular goods such as an automobile (along with its model, make, year, and color) as repayment to their parents, others focused more on their personal choices of academic majors and future careers. Similar to the automobile, the objective of selecting a career is an act of consuming a particular status-laden product. Selecting a career is deeply embedded in fulfilling expectations of one's parents as well as one's community. The act of migration, parental difficulty in adjustment, the children's years of education, and long hours at the family business at the expense of quality family time, are all investments or down payments towards the purchase of a new "home"; that is, belonging/acceptance in a new country.

However, consumption is not a solitary act. Consumption is a social relationship. According to bell hooks, it is *the* dominant social relationship in our society.[7] Its value and meaning are derived from the product consumed and the context in which it is consumed. It is a communal, political activity and an important expression of one's identity.[8] For Asian Americans, consumption is a provocative symbol of social citizenship, familial unity, and community identity. The intense pursuit of upward economic mobility in order to repay parental sacrifices and become a "normal" American family all contributes to this distinct process of consumption in Asian America.

Children of immigrant entrepreneurial families are particularly strategic in illustrating this process given their intense, direct connection to the family and the larger community on a daily basis through the family business. In this way, the small family business is a mediating institution that shapes, structures, and constrains interrelationships within the children's lives.[9] As a mediating institution, the business is a useful unit of analysis revealing how macro-level political and economic forces are brought to bear on micro-level relationships. The immigrant family business also plays a central role in the American ideology of meritocracy and equality. Given the deep connections between immigrant entrepreneurs and Asian Americans as the "model minority,"[10] these businesses and the Asian immigrants who run them often serve to symbolize an open society without a rigid class or race-based structure in which poor, uneducated immigrants with nothing but their determination and "family values" attain economic upward mobility and social acceptance in the United States. For many immigrants, consumption of particular items in a particular context is a powerful symbol of their identity as a "good" immigrant who contributes greater benefits than costs to the larger U.S. society. Given their profound and direct interaction with the family business and all the symbolism it embodies, these children of immigrants provide a unique opportunity to investigate the assumptions underlying immigrant adaptation and the powerful disciplinary effect of American Dream ideology upon the lives of the second generation.

This study focuses on two Asian American groups—Korean and Chinese Americans—that have some of the highest rates of entrepreneurialism in the United States.[11] In investigating the experiences of second generation Asian Americans through the lens of consumption, this study is not intended as a condemnation nor an endorsement of Asian Americans as consumers, but rather is a contribution towards a critical understanding of the role and significance of consumption in the exertion of social citizenship by children of immigrants in the United States.

The American Dream, Citizenship, and Race

For second generation Asian Americans, who find themselves bridging both Asia and America, consumption of status-laden material goods becomes an important initial step towards establishing one's social citizenship within the United States. Social citizenship embodies a distinct set of rights as "full members of society entitled to 'equal respect'" that go beyond civil and political rights.[12] Within a Welfare State, Nancy Fraser and Linda Gordon explain, this form of citizenship would imply an entitlement in which people get "social rights" not "handouts."[13] The basis for Fraser and Gordon's definition is found in T. H. Marshall's 1949 essay "Citizenship and Social Class," wherein social citizenship is the final stage of modern citizenship that goes beyond the guarantee of economic security but is also "a share in the full social heritage and to live the life of a civilized being according to the standards prevailing in the society."[14] This sense of legitimacy and belonging is the ultimate goal for many Asian Americans (and immigrants in general), particularly perhaps because it is so elusive.

The achievement of social citizenship rights is deeply interwoven with consumption because "successful" immigrant adaptation is narrowly prescribed in economic terms wherein personal wealth and income become the primary indicator of adjustment. Economic gains are presumed to precede the next stage of true acceptance. The second generation plays a crucial role in this scenario in that they become the primary evidence of their parents' successful or unsuccessful incorporation to the United States.[15] In addition, evidence of this wealth must be routinely displayed. This ideology presents a singular notion of success: economic upward mobility.[16] In this way, the proof of social citizenship or "belonging" is presented through possession of material goods that symbolize that one contributes to rather than burdens the United States—thereby making one a "good" (versus "bad") immigrant.[17]

Implicit in this American Dream is the promise of American Democracy and equality.[18] For people of color, who comprise the majority of the current immigrant population, there is an underlying expectation of reprieve from racial discrimination through class mobility and accompanying privilege. In other words, by purchasing the American Dream of "single-family houses, quiet tree-lined streets, and good schools for their children"[19] with funds earned from long working hours, immigrants expect equal opportunity (at least for their children) for upward mobility regardless of their race or class. The children of these immigrants have even greater expectations of equality than their parents' generation, who expect differential treatment based on race to some degree given their foreign status and their homeland claims to another country. As products of the U.S. education system, mass media, and the Civil Rights movement, young children of immigrants—as Americans—understand that they should receive equal treatment and opportunities.

These expectations are based on social rather than legal definitions of citizenship.[20] Citizenship fulfills both legal and political functions in providing privileges to some at the expense of others.[21] It is a normative ideology that dictates how members of a given nation-state should behave depending upon particular social markers including race and gender.[22] Citizenship, then, is an important perspective from which to understand the unequal power structure and the relegation of individuals to particular spaces within this hierarchy based upon their race, class, and gender.[23] In addition, consumption becomes a central site from which to observe the maintenance and reproduction of citizenship, or more specifically, *social* citizenship. Similarly, scholars[24] have utilized the concept of citizenship as a tool to investigate the boundary transformations within societies and communities. In this regard, social citizenship is a pivotal lens through which to understand the shifting boundaries of belonging, entitlement, and participation of Asian Americans in U.S. society.

The adaptation strategy of the "good immigrant" is a crucial example of social citizenship claims-making.[25] For instance, despite the fact that Asian immigrants were restricted from legal citizenship until the 1950s, Japanese Americans were careful to present themselves as socially and economically well adjusted (i.e., politically passive and financially independent) in the face of racist anti-Asian hostilities. Such social practices are certainly understandable, given Executive Order 9066, which imprisoned approximately 120,000 persons of Japanese ancestry in concentration camps in the United States during World War II.[26] Given that the majority of those imprisoned were U.S.-born, it is clear that legal inclusion does not necessarily imply social inclusion and, consequently, equal protection under the law. The forced incarceration of Japanese Americans is a dramatic, historical illustration of differential citizenship rights based upon race. It is also an important example of the historical legacy of the U.S. Constitution, which, in its infancy, restricted citizenship to white men of property.[27]

For those who do not possess the appropriate race (white), class (of property), and gender (men), making a claim upon the state is a conscious struggle. This is the case for Asian Americans even today. They continue to be regarded as perpetual foreigners regardless of their immigration status. Citizenship is a privilege or an assumed right for some, but for others it is an elusive status that requires continuous effort to establish oneself as deserving of equal rights and opportunities. For Asian Americans, class status becomes the central route from which to establish one's right to make claims upon the state. Within this understanding, there is a central assumption that the greater one's wealth, the greater one's protection from racism and bigotry—that you will become "American" and no longer foreign by establishing yourself as (economically) worthy. Upward economic mobility is perhaps the most strenuously applied measure of social citizenship.[28]

Since 9 / 11 and the second war in Iraq, competitive flag-waving or "coercive patriotism" has been at an all-time high. One's patriotism, it seems, is best exemplified by provocative displays of wealth.[29] While anyone can post a picture of the U.S. flag on her/his automobile or home during times of foreigner angst, patriotism is taken to another level when that flag is posted on a mansion in a gated community or on a Hummer—it is, in fact, redundant.[30] The association of wealth and patriotism is a strongly held American conviction. In times of nativistic fervor, immigrants and those who *look* "foreign" feel the expectation of some form of patriotic display most painfully. The everyday pressure to show one's sole allegiance is heightened during times of war and nationalistic hostilities.

One's class status is, in effect, a citizenship test that indicates whether one is a "dependent," burdensome immigrant or a "deserving," model minority. However, as various Asian American scholars have so eloquently argued, this "choice" is a false one, in that this notion of a model minority does not imply full citizenship rights but is rather a secondary one afforded to those minorities who "behave" and stay in their designated social space. Those who benefit from this unequal system understand the American Dream for immigrants/foreigners as different from that for "real Americans." There is a double standard. This imperialistic ideology denotes a particular space for immigrants/foreigners and people of color within a racial hierarchy. As perpetual foreigners, second generation Asian Americans who expect more than their parents are "bad," ungrateful immigrants/foreigners who do not deserve to be here when there are so many others in the world who need to be "rescued."

The American Dream, then, is a capitalistic, free market ideology in which only those who can pay the price of admission may enter. Interestingly, U.S.-based ethnocentrism lays claim to the successes of those Asian Americans who have found upward economic mobility by separating the American from the Asian. In other words, economic success is attributed solely to the opportunities garnered through the United States and its American Democracy. A more nuanced socio-historical understanding shows that upward social or economic mobility of children of immigrants is, in fact, the hard-won struggle of children following Asian (e.g., Korean or Chinese) based ideals as passed down by their immigrant parents and communities. In reality, their achievements are made *despite* the barriers in occupational structure and racial/gender/class discrimination imposed by U.S. society; it is the resources brought from the emigrant country that play a key role in the adjustment within the host country.

The findings from this study support the idea that career choices of second generation Asian American high school and college students are, in fact, an act of conspicuous consumption, in that these decisions are made in a conscious effort to establish their own and their family's worth, belonging, and acceptance into U.S. society. Second generation Asian Americans find themselves in the middle of a paradox of national identity. They are perpetually foreign[31] due to their race and yet are promised that if they just worked as hard and as quietly as their parents, they will be offered equal opportunity (unlike their parents, who were immigrants/foreign). This paradox gives rise to yet another problem for the second generation—how to reconcile the fact that you are benefiting from or buying into the same system that discriminates against your parents? In this case, one must either justify the discrimination (perhaps by redefining or misnaming it to avoid the psychic struggle) or fight/contest it. The respondents in this study exhibited both responses.

As children of immigrants, these respondents' stories about their struggle for acceptance and success are crucial for building a more nuanced understanding of immigrants and social citizenship. Alejandro Portes describes the experiences of the second generation as a "strategic research site," where general theoretical contributions are derived with "unusual clarity."[32] In this case, the pattern of citizenship claims-making through consumption that is exercised by many Asian American children of immigrants highlights the contradictions that result from the intersection of democratic ideals with non-democratic realities. The American Dream ideology, however noble and attractive, is an impossible goal for many minorities given the real race/ethnic, gender, and class based barriers. Instead, the American Dream is a fictive, disciplinary measure that keeps in place normative, unequal social structures by enticing marginalized groups with the possibility of full participation. Asian American children of immigrant entrepreneurs, as subjects who embody the myths of the model minority and the American Dream, are ideal for exploring the realities of this paradox.

"I Shop, Therefore I Am": Consumption,
Conformity, and Difference

Journalist and social commentator Roger Rosenblatt writes that " . . . it
is the perpetual and relentless round of having and yearning that drives the
system" of Western capitalism.[33] He states that "[t]he thrill of the present
drags you into the want of the past and then propels you into prayers for
the future."[34] Rosenblatt alludes to the complexity (and the addictive
nature[35]) of consumption as a social issue. Rather than taking a dry, utili-
tarian approach to consumption that incorrectly views shopping patterns as
random distribution of individual tastes and preferences, this study takes
seriously the social implications that motivate the never-ending trips to the
mall.[36] This section outlines some of the social dilemmas entrenched in
consumption and the prevailing role of consumption in defining one's
identity, nationality, and citizenship.

One of the strongest arguments against a consumer-based society is its
impact in reproducing race and class hierarchies. Juliet Schor writes,
"Spending patterns not only reflect a structure of social inequality but also
reproduce it. . . . Socially visible, or 'conspicuous,' consumption is a major
strategy used by high-status groups to keep themselves intact."[37] Schor's
argument is an extension of Thorstein Veblen's classic theory of conspicuous consumption, which held that consumption of particular luxuries was
an act of marking boundaries between those who are superior and those
who are inferior. In addition, such conspicuous consumption is also an
important tool used by those lower on the social status hierarchy, but for a
different purpose, given their relative powerlessness. Veblen noted that consumptive boundaries were powerful social control mechanisms: "On pain
of forfeiting their good name and their self-respect in case of failure, they
must conform to the accepted code, at least in appearance."[38]

Of crucial significance in this analysis is an understanding of the *rela-*
tional nature of consumption that requires a hierarchical structure, in
which one must be poor for another to be rich. As such, consumption is a
political act based upon social relationships that reinforce class and race
boundaries. In addition, consumption is a sort of competitive sport.[39]
While some cultural critics have argued that the postmodern nature of
today's culture has diminished the impact of consumption in structuring

social class,[40] Schor and others[41] have argued otherwise. In fact, Schor contends that consumption is at an all-time high and that the competition is more intense than ever.[42] Rather than fracturing and diminishing the significance of consumptive goods, increased globalization of capital has increased the standard of the "good life" as well as expanded the number of players in this competitive sport. More and more people around the world want/need to "keep up with the Joneses."

Children of immigrants find themselves in a difficult position in trying to compete to become a member of the reference group (i.e., white, middle-class) that has historically marginalized their presence. As adolescents / young adults and perceived foreigners, the Chinese and Korean Americans in this study experience a paradox in which they must find or create their true "self" while at the same time conform to the socially condoned ideal of the "good" immigrant. Consumption becomes an important, acceptable venue from which to accomplish this complex feat.

Through consumption of particular well-known, status-laden objects—cars, clothes, careers—these children of immigrants are internalizing/digesting their difference or foreignness. By absorbing the difference that once marginalized them, they attempt to re-center themselves as "normal." Consumption, then, is a vital act for the sake of full citizenship, in that it is difference that construes Asian Americans as the "other" and "foreign" and therefore ineligible for full social inclusion. Lisa Lowe states that the American contract of citizenship (particularly for Asian immigrant women) is essentially contradictory, in that while the state presents itself as a democratic, unified body in which all subjects are granted equal access, it also demands that differences—of race, class, gender, and locality—be subordinated in order to qualify for membership.[43]

Consumption is also an act of ritual that is an important part of one's identity formation. In this study, I approach consumption as a ritual that is tailored specifically, in this case, to the experiences of second generation Asian Americans.[44] In this way, the social process or ritual of consuming is as important as what is being consumed. One consumes in order to *be*. Ironically, it is through this familiar experience that one finds individuality or difference. It is in this understanding of difference, used as a creative tool, that uniqueness is identified. This state of *being* or finding one's true self, then, is about finding a home or community—a place of effortless acceptance—to belong. For children of immigrants, the process of conspicuous consumption of goods is an effort towards finding one's "real" self or place (i.e., one's "difference") while at the same time participating in a communal, socially accepted (i.e., "normal") ritual.

However, within the reality of this difference that is highlighted through the act of consumption, there remains a central issue—power. While consuming difference can function as an act of ownership, and in that way as a significant presentation of individuality, the act remains within the confines of an acceptable, "American" ideology. The acceptable perimeters of consumptive behavior limit what kind of difference may be consumed in the first place.[45] Consumptive patterns display unequal power relationships. For example, in describing an "inversion" of consumption in which middle-class suburban white children mimic the "style" of inner-city Black children, Kotlowitz argues that the fashion bond between the ghetto and suburb is a false one.[46] The similarities in consumptive patterns are superficial, whereas the differences in poverty, racism, and social isolation are real. Consumptive similarities mask the underlying unequal power relationships. This is evident among the Asian American young adults in this study as they discuss their limited number of acceptable career choices. Within this model, there are clearly defined boundaries limiting the extent to which one can express his/her differences.

But, can the act of consumption—in any form—alter the power dynamics of society? If in fact, as bell hooks contends, "white racism, imperialism, and sexist domination prevail by courageous consumption," and that "by eating the Other . . . one asserts power and privilege,"[47] can the Other undo the unequal power structure by doing what the powerful have done to the powerless (i.e., by eating/consuming the Norm)? In other words, can Asian Americans, through consumption of normative behavior and products eat/eliminate their own difference and thereby normalize their identity? This would require that enough room for creativity and subversion exist within the boundaries of consumer society to alter the system itself. Or is it the case, as Audre Lorde so eloquently stated, "The masters' tools will never dismantle the master's house?"

On this question, Horkheimer and Adorno would side with Lorde. They argue that, rather than emancipation, the mass culture industry has as its central goal obedience to the social hierarchy.[48] This goal is achieved through perpetual promises of pleasure. In this way, consumption is the pursuit of a rather elaborately contrived illusion. Therefore, the consumer is tricked into behavior that in the long run reinforces the trickery itself. Interestingly, this process of consumption has a cyclical dimension in that the more one consumes, the greater one's appetite for yet more consumption. Resistance through consumption is a contentious proposition that remains largely unconvincing, in part because the structure of consumption requires the perpetuation of unmet needs. The fulfillment of its promise spells its own demise.

Asian Americans, as members of an "Other," or marginal, community, are in a precarious situation. Difference is a ghostly matter[49] that silently follows Asian Americans in their pursuit of full social participation. It is a social reality with tangible consequences that most of us fear to fully address. Similar to the "fear of falling," or downward mobility, exhibited by the white middle class,[50] Asian Americans find themselves standing on a "fault line,"[51] vulnerable to the slightest quake or change in social boundaries between "us" and "them." Their social role as a mythical model minority requires that they continuously exhibit their patriotism or their deservingness of social citizenship through consumptive displays. Otherwise, they may fall into the "bad" immigrant category and experience even greater limitations on their social citizenship claims. However, many Asian Americans are aware of the class-based frictions that this show of citizenship causes within the community, as well as the race-based competition among ethnic minorities to climb the hierarchical status ladder that reinforces inequality in U.S. society. Asian Americans, then, consume in distinctive ways to display their identity, nationality, and citizenship within specific socially sanctioned boundaries. This study will pay particular attention to career decisions as acts of consumption. Implicit within this scenario is a guiding principle that prohibits the extension of these boundaries beyond themselves so that the inequities that structure consumptive patterns remain undisturbed.

Asian Immigrant Entrepreneur as an "American" Ideology

Asian immigrant entrepreneurs inhabit a particular ideological and symbolic space in the United States. Entrepreneurs have become an important symbolic representation of Asian America.[52] For instance, during the 1992 Los Angeles rebellion, journalists repeatedly identified Korean Americans on the whole as prosperous ghetto shopkeepers.[53] They did so despite the fact that the majority of Korean Americans do not own small businesses.[54] The attraction towards this image of Asian Americans as immigrant entrepreneurs is twofold. First, this image conveniently confirms the myth of Asian Americans as the model minority. Second, this image renders Asian Americans as easily "consumable."

As a model minority, Asian Americans represent the American Dream of meritocracy and democracy—the idea that anyone regardless of race, class, or gender status has an equal opportunity to work hard and be rewarded for their labor through economic upward mobility. It is ironic that the powerful draw of this myth is its promise of belonging or acceptance as a "real" American, but at the same time, this myth is culturally based upon designated "Asian" traits. Therefore, one must be a good "Asian" in order to be considered a good "American." What is significant here is that both of these cultural categories are socially constructed. Claire Jean Kim[55] argues that this model minority construction socially defines Asian Americans as an inferior "other." According to Kim, this process of racial "othering" is essential in upholding racial power, or the systemic self-reproduction of the racial status quo. In addition, she explains, racial power "operates not only by reproducing racial categories and meanings per se but by reproducing them in the form of a distinct racial order."[56] "Each group is racialized relative to other groups, so that Asian immigrants and their children are "triangulated" both as inferior to whites and superior to Blacks and as permanently foreign and inassimilable."[57] This racialization of an inferior other is necessary in presenting Asian Americans/immigrants as consumable—that is, easily digestible and marketable. Similar to the marketing of Latinos described by Arlene Dávila, Asian Americans as consumers are the only "safe" or acceptable form of expressing ethnic differences. Ethnicity as demonstrated by consumption is a sanitized, uncomplicated, and depoliticized version that is easily (mis)understood as a kind of food, music, or clothing.[58]

As a form of American ideology, this consumable rendering of difference via the Asian immigrant entrepreneur makes for a more palatable version of U.S. history. In this regard, Yen Le Espiritu differentiates the rose-colored history of immigration from the history of conquest and annexation.[59] Espiritu makes a powerful point by connecting the history of Asian Americans to that of Native Americans, African Americans, and Latinos.[60] In this historical rendering, the differential inclusion of Asian Americans— like that of other racial ethnic minorities—comes to symbolize the colonial past and present of the American Empire. The ethnic differences are no longer so easy to digest or market within this context.

However, the social forces that perpetuate the immigration narrative, as opposed to that of imperialism, are ever-present. The ideological construction that equated American integration of new immigrants through the linkage of democracy with the consumption of goods during the last turn of the century continues to reign. In this construction, Asian immigrant entrepreneurs play an important role in illustrating the ideological connection between democracy and consumption. Aihwa Ong argues that the taken-for-grant association of self-discipline, consumer power, and human entrepreneurial capital with whiteness makes Asian Americans seemingly more compatible with U.S. citizenship ideals.[61] The fallacy embedded in this rationale is that it is a promise that is never realized. It functions, and has functioned, as a "carrot" for the continuous perpetuation of the American ideology of democracy. Thus, despite the fact that Asian Americans, as the model minority, have the symbolic resources for citizenship, they remain suspect as they ride the fine line between model minority and "yellow peril."[62]

In this tenuous predicament, there is compelling pressure to establish one's "worth" or "patriotism" through participatory democracy via consumption, so that the expansion of consumer choice is equated with the spread of democracy and the purchase of an automobile is transformed into a civic duty intended to defend "our" way of life. For second generation Asian American consumers, the burden of proving one's "Americanism" requires that they display affluence in a particular way that displays their desire to be "American" and at the same time, remain in their triangulated, inferior position as racialized foreigners. This requires that they display consumptive patterns that present difference or otherness in quaint, non-threatening, and digestible forms. In effect, they must try to climb up the racial hierarchy through upward economic mobility but never actually disrupt the hierarchy itself. Entrepreneurialism, by embodying the central criterion for citizenship, becomes an important lesson in this mainstream ideology of democracy and upward mobility.

However, the everyday reality of immigrant entrepreneurialism is a difficult one. The romantic notion of small family businesses ignores the existence of social structures that limit one's self-employment options, including the ability to mobilize resources such as capital and labor. In addition, quality of education, racial and gender discrimination, intense competition within a small market, and difficult working conditions pose significant barriers to successful self-employment.

Fifty percent of all small businesses fail in the first two years. In addition, those that succeed are not people who do so to escape poverty. In his study of Korean immigrant entrepreneurs, In-Jin Yoon reports that personal motivation for business ownership and ability to mobilize capital, information, and workers are both essential for entrepreneurial success.[63] He writes that "businesses that were started solely for the purposes of creating a job for oneself were very likely to fail."[64] On average, a small business hires two seasonal employees—hardly a new source of job creation. Given these odds, the chances that a person in poverty will succeed in self-employment are very slim, no matter how hard one works. In fact, a failed attempt may result in greater financial troubles. Abelmann and Lie explain: " . . . many Korean Americans opened shops because they were shut out of white-collar jobs and found small businesses to be more desirable than manual labor, while others, especially in the 1980s, came to the United States planning to open shops because their prospects in South Korea were limited."[65] For many successful entrepreneurs, their business is a result of *downward mobility*.

The strong presence of immigrant entrepreneurs in the United States is generally understood as a result of the "productive" use of human and physical capital (particularly the use of unpaid family labor).[66] However, the measurable benefits of self-employment are debatable.[67] Given the continued currency of the rags-to-riches narrative—which deeply imbues the immigrant family business with sentimental notions of family values, upward mobility, and the model minority myth—the uncertainty, vulnerability, and everyday stresses of growing up in an immigrant entrepreneurial family have largely gone unnoticed. As Abelmann and Lie point out, "the uncritical celebration of Korean American entrepreneurial success or the faulty generalizations that all Korean immigrants are successful obfuscates the problems facing Korean Americans."[68] In In-Jin Yoon's study of contemporary Korean immigrants, the experience of Asian immigrant entrepreneurs is described in this way: "On balance, it is a bittersweet livelihood, entailing enormous physical, psychological, familial, and social costs to generate a moderate income."[69]

Outline of the Book

This book critically examines the process in which Korean American and Chinese American children of entrepreneurial immigrants struggle to define themselves as Americans. Central to this investigation is the question of *why* Asian Americans are made to prove their "Americanness" and *how* they do so—rather than the usual question of whether or not they are American. I argue that Korean and Chinese American children of immigrants are expected and obligated to assert and reassert their presence as "good" (i.e., economically beneficial) within a contested political context that is, at best, ambivalent towards the growing number of racial ethnic immigrants. The experiences of children raised in Asian immigrant small family businesses are particularly insightful, given their role as epitomizing the quintessentially American narrative of individual success and upward mobility. And, within these narratives, the primacy of conspicuous consumption of status symbols is evident in the children's efforts to establish their social citizenship.

The subsequent chapters delve into the everyday work and family experiences of these Korean American and Chinese American children of Asian immigrants entrepreneurs. Chapter Two begins by examining the historical and social context of Korean and Chinese migration to the United States. This chapter discusses some of the differences and similarities between the two ethnic groups represented by the respondents in this study. I also outline the general state of Asian immigrant enterprise. In Chapter Three, I explore how the pursuit of a "normal American family" is an effort to "contain" the difference that marks the experiences of Asian Americans as marginal. This "containment" is achieved through consumptive means as the children negotiate the delicate boundary between work and family. Chapter Four investigates the impact of the family business on family life through the adult children's retelling of their early childhood memories of playing and working at the family store. These accounts reveal a complex, commodified social environment of blurred work and family boundaries in which children grow up too fast and, as young adults, never age. Chapter Five concentrates on the children's immigration narratives. Here, I argue that these narratives are American constructions that function to normalize their presence and are, therefore, fundamental to understanding why and how second generation Asian Americans feel compelled to remind others of their legitimate existence in the United States. Chapter Six argues that career decisions are the most important form of conspicuously displayed consumption for Asian American children, given their burden to represent the success or failure of immigrant "adaptation" in the United States. The second generation negotiates between various obligations, expectations, and sacrifices in order to build the social capital necessary to ensure upward mobility not only for themselves but also for the first generation. By displaying evidence of attaining the American Dream, the children hope to finally be treated as the Americans that they are. Finally, Chapter Seven concludes with a discussion of consumption and its continuing prevailing presence in determining the direction of American democracy.

Methods

I conducted more than a hundred in-depth interviews with Chinese and Korean adolescents and young adults, their families, and respective ethnic community members. Eighty-eight of these interviews were with children and thirty-four with family members (including parents, aunts, uncles) and community leaders. Seventy-one of the eighty-eight young adult and adolescent respondents grew up as part of a household that owned a family

TABLE I.I

Number of Entrepreneurial and Non-entrepreneurial
Respondents by Ethnicity

Respondents	Chinese Am.	Korean Am.	Total
Entrepreneurial	35	36	71
Non-entrepreneurial	10	7	17
Total	43	45	88

business. There were a variety of types of family businesses (see Appendix A) and a varying degree of individual involvement with the business. While not a perfect fit, the majority of the businesses were "typical" ethnic immigrant, small family businesses requiring intense family labor, rarely employing more than five non-family workers, operating at low economies of scale, and located in urban communities with affordable overhead costs (i.e., rent). Included in the study were a few small family businesses that require a greater input of social capital (such as English language acquisition), perform a "skilled" form of labor, operate in a more stable primary product sector with larger economies of scale, and require less family labor. However, these more "professional" businesses were located in small storefronts within ethnic or immigrant communities. Finally, there were seventeen additional respondents comprising a comparison sample of non-entrepreneurial Chinese and Korean children of immigrants of the same age and class. The numerical breakdown is shown in Table I.I.

Fifty-one of the informants were female and thirty-seven were male. Their ages ranged from 15 to 26 years old. Only eight respondents were adolescents (15–17 years of age) and the remaining eighty were young adults (18–26 years of age). The small sample of adolescents was drawn as a comparison case to address potential developmental questions. Although this study focuses on young adults, the young adult participants are referred to as "children" in certain contexts to highlight their relationship with their parents.

The initial interviews were conducted face-to-face or on the telephone and lasted one to three hours. Follow-up interviews that ranged from thirty minutes to two hours were conducted as needed. In addition to the in-depth interviews, focus groups and participant observation were utilized. Through fieldwork, I became acquainted with a number of the respondents' parents, siblings, and extended family members. For the face-to-face interviews, I visited their homes, schools, and businesses. In addition, I conducted three sets of focus group interviews, after which I conducted individual follow-up interviews. I found these groups fruitful in sharpening the individual interview instrument and identifying the more pressing issues and prevalent themes. The focus groups were especially helpful in eliciting active participation among the high school students.

Initially, I met with ethnic community and business leaders, attended meetings, and made individual appointments. As cordial as they were, they were reluctant to provide access to their own families and to the families of members. While there are significant limitations in a snowball sampling method, a random sample was not feasible for this particular population. I had at first attempted to systematically interview the children of parents who were members of an official ethnic-specific business organization (such as the Korean American Dry Cleaners Association), but these organizations proved to be strict gatekeepers. The few interviews I was allowed using this method yielded limited data. In those sessions, I was forced to interview the adolescents/young adults in the presence of their parents, aunts, uncles, and whoever else happened to drop by. In these situations, the parents (particularly the fathers) dominated the discussion and the children merely acted as interpreters. Siblings were also a difficult group to interview. Most siblings were reluctant to speak with me. Most of them were younger than the respondents and still embedded in the family business, unlike their older sister or brother, who had left for college. They were generally polite in their refusal, and some candidly told me that it was too painful to talk about their feelings towards the business and their parents. They described a "suffocating" family life and felt unable to verbalize their experience.

I deliberately incorporated multiple research methods—in-depth interviews, focus groups, and participant observation using both snowball and random sampling—to avoid the pitfall of making unwarranted assumptions about groups based solely on the observation of a few individuals. Also, my theoretical considerations were derived from careful inductive or "grounded" theory,[70] which starts with observed data and, in stages, develops substantiated generalizations. For analysis purposes, each interview, including focus groups, was tape recorded with the respondent's permission. I preceded each interview by providing a short description of the research project and explicitly notifying respondents of their confidentiality.[71] Each tape was transcribed for content analysis. After an initial perusal of the transcribed text, I initiated an open coding process.[72] This coding process helped me to identify concepts and themes that fit the existing data. In the preliminary coding process, I looked for inconsistencies, repetitions, and other patterns in the text. I then developed a template or analysis guide using the core interview questions. The template was then applied to the text. This method of analysis discerns themes, patterns, and interrelationships in an interpretive, rather than statistical, manner. This method permits the investigator to revise after encountering the text. In addition, two research assistants independently recoded the data using the initial template to double-check the reliability of my analysis.

In the beginning I did not seek members of any specific Asian American community. However, those who responded were almost exclusively Chinese or Korean American. This response is consistent with self-employment rates in general. Both Korean Americans and Chinese Americans rank above the national average for self-employment.[73]

Even though the ethnic diversity of respondents was limited, there was great variation in types of businesses (see Appendix A). Early in the research process, I decided not to narrow the type of business. I found striking similarities across the diverse individuals, regardless of the type of family business. Restaurants, for example, on average ranged in size from six to fourteen tables. They rarely had more than one or two non-family employees. This was generally true of the other businesses as well. Also, the respondents did not represent any one region (see Appendix B). The majority lived in the Midwest and California. Upon careful comparison of hometowns, there were surprisingly few differences in the respondents' experiences, regardless of location. Instead, their identity as Asian Americans and their common experiences of growing up at the family store were so pervasive that they appeared to minimize the regional differences.

The majority of the respondents were not born in the United States.

Technically, these respondents would be considered *1.5 generation* rather than second generation.[74] However, the vast majority arrived at such a young age that the lines differentiating 1.5 and second generation blur. The families in this study immigrated to the United States between the early 1970s and mid-1980s. They entered the country with family visas generally with the help of an extended relative, usually an aunt or uncle. These contacts not only helped them to adjust culturally, but also provided them entrée into entrepreneurialism. Many times, the father arrived first to establish some stability. After finding an apartment and a job, he would send for the rest of the immediate family. There was usually a two- to four-year separation from the father. The vast majority of the respondents came from two-parent households, but nine respondents out of the seventy-one entrepreneurial children had parents who were either divorced or widowed. Also, apart from two of the Chinese American families, the rest of the families had no experience working in or running a small business prior to immigration.

All of the young adults in this sample were in college or college-bound at the time of the study. The absence of respondents who did not go to college or had no intention of going is a limitation of this study. However, the respondents in this study were enrolled in a diverse mix of colleges ranging from community colleges to state universities to private Ivy League universities. Almost all of them classified themselves as middle class, regardless of their family's actual income level. This was not surprising, given the persistent efforts of these Chinese and Korean American children of immigrants to legitimize their place in the United States as "normal" Americans.

In the next chapter, I outline the historical background and social context of Chinese and Korean immigrant entrepreneurs and their children. I address the disciplinary nature of the American Dream for the children of immigrants within the commodified environment of immigrant enterprises. I also illustrate the social conditions on which second generation incorporation is predicated.

CHAPTER TWO

Minding the Family Store

Our destination is fixed on the perpetual motion of search. Fixed in its
perpetual exile.
—Theresa Hak Kyung Cha[1]

In his presidential address at the annual meeting of the Immigration
History Society in 1997, Roger Daniels noted that the entire historiography
of American immigration has almost exclusively focused on Europeans.
Until very recently, Asian immigration was written off as an aberration.[2] In
the last two decades, research on Asian migration and Asian immigrants has
burgeoned into a central position from which to understand contemporary
migration in general.[3] In the period since the passage of immigration
reforms in 1965, which did away with a national quota system, immigrants
from Asia and Latin America have come to comprise the majority of newcomers to the United States.[4] In addition, the children of immigrants comprise 20 percent of all youth in the United States, making them the fastest-
growing segment of the country's total population of children less than
eighteen years of age.[5] Within the Asian American community, 90 percent
of all children are immigrants or the children of immigrants.[6]

For Asian America, this new post-1965 migration was a watershed event
that brought fundamental changes to its communities. Leading up to this
historic moment, heightened awareness of the xenophobic and nativist
nature of immigration laws—which were enacted from 1875 to 1934 explicitly to control the number of Chinese, Japanese, Korean, Asian Indian, and
Filipino immigrants—in conjunction with wartime alliances formed in the
1940s, finally led to the erosion of these exclusionary immigration policies.[7]

In fact, as Sucheng Chan notes, discriminatory laws such as the Chinese Exclusion Act of 1882—which was the first congressional measure to limit immigrants on the basis of race or color—were what set Asian immigrants apart from European immigrants. Chan argues that while all immigrant communities, regardless of their national origin, experienced some form of prejudice and violence at one time or another, the first wave of Asian immigrants encountered laws that aimed to deprive them, specifically, of their means of livelihood, restrict their social mobility, and deny them political power.[8] These early legislative measures have had a profound effect on Asian American communities in the current, second, wave, in that the development of a native-born second generation was stunted. Chan writes that for many immigrant groups, upward mobility was an intergenerational phenomenon and that the Asian American community, as a whole, experienced a significant loss in time and potential as a result of eight decades of exclusion between 1882 and 1965.[9] The Asian American community was virtually at a standstill during these long years. It was not until these restrictions were lifted that a significant number of second generation Asian Americans entered the scene and revitalized the community.

Given the youth of today's Asian immigrant population, the assumption that the second generation would play a crucial role in advancing the mobility and social citizenship status for Asian America has increasingly been put to the test. Complicating this analysis is the growing economic bifurcation of incoming Asian immigrants. For instance, in her study of Indian American youth culture, Sunaina M. Maira intertwines the mobility aspirations of second generation Asian Indians within the U.S. economy in which they find themselves and concludes that the presumed Asian American "model minority" has little relevance for the substantial numbers of working- and lower-middle-class people in their community. The challenges of growing up for the second generation, then, encompass not only the individual-level concerns about adaptation but also larger, societal-level concerns about the political economy. Consequently, studies that position the experiences of the second generation within some critical consideration of the larger historical, social, political, or economic conditions stand out. In addition to Maira's work, Vivian Louie's rejuvenating discussion of the well-worn "model minority" myth as a form of discipline also illustrates this critical positioning: " . . . the model-minority myth was an effective way of disciplining such claims of inequality without ever naming the dominant group's vested interest in the existing paradigm of race rela-tions."[10] Louie makes clear that this myth about Asian Americans was introduced purposefully in 1966 at the height of the Civil Rights move-ment. The myth was used to "discipline" claims of injustice during a time of tremendous racial anxiety.

Similar to Aihwa Ong's definition of capitalist discipline, the model minority myth promotes the "enforced and induced compliance"[11] of the second generation with specific political, social, and economic objectives. The term *discipline* makes central the power of institutions in maintaining a hierarchical structure in which Asian Americans are compelled to adhere. A standard treatment of adaptation, on the other hand, narrowly focuses on the second generation as a compilation of outcome measures that indi-cate how well they perform on given tests of "Americanness" (school per-formance, English language acquisition, etc.) with little critique of the measurements themselves. Likewise, I argue that conspicuous consumption is one such disciplinary measure for second generation Asian Americans. The notion of discipline provides a more critical approach than adaptation, by focusing on the social inequality that compels the children of immi-grants to continually prove their worth/patriotism despite the long history of Asian American presence in the United States.

This chapter provides a historical and social context for the experiences of the Korean and Chinese American children of immigrants discussed in this book. I first position their experiences within the larger scholarly liter-ature on immigration. Second, I show how Korean and Chinese Americans, despite their significant historical and cultural differences, forge a strong, collective Asian American identity. Third, I provide background information regarding the family businesses of the children in this study and outline the development of the Asian immigrant enterprise in general.

Developing a Critical Approach for the Next Generation

Research on the Asian American second generation is relatively new.[12] Recently, there have been a growing number of studies on immigrant children and the second generation.[13] However, much of this literature tends to stay within the familiar construction of adaptation and assimilation concerns. The usual questions that measured assimilation of immigrants of an earlier era are posed once again to a new generation, coming largely from different parts of the globe in distinctive economic and political conditions.

That is not to imply that theories of immigration have remained entirely static. On the contrary, they have changed markedly certainly since Oscar Handlin wrote *The Uprooted* in 1951.[14] What Handlin explained as simply an "injection" of foreigners into a larger, established society has evolved into a more sophisticated explanation of immigration in which the *process* is emphasized.[15] This is evident among a number of contemporary theorists including Patricia Fernandez-Kelly, Richard Schauffler, Alejandro Portes, Ivan Light, and Edna Bonacich, who interpret the process of immigration as a movement of labor.[16] Incorporating Saskia Sassen's[17] work on transnational labor markets, these authors conclude that the continuing trend towards economic globalization will increase the demand for immigrant labor and increase the formation of transnational markets. From these studies came the first wave of research on the children of the "new" post-1965 immigrants.

Using this backdrop of the world economy, Alejandro Portes convincingly argues that neglecting the second generation is detrimental to understanding the long-term consequences of immigration. He underscores the use of immigrants as an "abundant source of labor to fuel economic growth and restrain the power of domestic workers"[18] and notes the complete neglect of the workers' children by the employers. He notes that the potential consequences of the children's maladjustment as a result of these forms of labor rest entirely on immigrant families, many of whom may already have limited resources.

In these important studies, children were finally linked to the outside world. For instance, Ruben Rumbaut's[19] work on immigrant children showed that socio-economic status measures such as downward mobility and economic stress produce low psychological well-being for adolescents and increase parent-child conflicts. Consequently, family businesses as economic institutions are understood to affect children's lives significantly. In addition, many small entrepreneurial families experience a greater dependence upon unpaid family labor and other forms of informal economic strategies during uncertain economic times.

However, the main purpose of these studies on immigrant children appears to be the investigation of the immigrant adaptation process apart from the actual perspective—or subjectivity—of the children themselves. David Manuel Hernandez and Evelyn Nakano Glenn critique this standard focus on adaptation as a "status-attainment framework" that emphasizes individual mobility and assumes the "necessity of immigrants fitting into a preexisting hierarchy."[20] Both Portes and Rumbaut stress the potential economic benefit and cost associated with the second generation as the primary reason why we should find them a valuable group to study. This focus keeps in place the standard assumption about the way in which immigration studies are conducted and what are understood to be the appropriate research questions. The focus remains the "good" or "bad" adaptation of immigrants, to the neglect of the social institutions that produce the unequal conditions of adaptation. Interestingly, earlier studies of adaptation based upon the experiences of immigrants from Europe have been critiqued for their lack of explanatory power in capturing today's immigrant experiences.[21] Even so, the same questions are applied once again.

Yen Espiritu argues for a more critical study of immigration. She stresses the need to understand immigration "not as a site for assessing the acceptability of the immigrants, but as a site for critiquing state claims of liberal democracy and cultural inclusion."[22] Toward this end, Espiritu attempts to disrupt the "mythistory" of the United States that "valorizes the linear narratives of immigration, assimilation, and adulthood."[23] She begins this disruption by arguing that immigrants are "differentially included" into U.S. society. She defines this as a process "whereby a group of people is deemed integral to the nation's economy, culture, identity, and power—but integral only or precisely because of their designated subordinate standing."[24] This narrative reconstruction of immigration highlights the necessity of immigrants as secondary members of society. This, then, provides a much needed critical assessment of the role of immigrants in constructing a national narrative of equality and democracy. Questions of assimilation and adaptation give way to concerns with power, inequality, and citizenship.

For those who are truly accorded the full protection of citizenship, there is no need for such proof of compliance. The continued focus on the adaptation rather than the discipline of children of immigrants, who are legally and socially Americans, exoticizes their experiences as, once again, foreigners trying to adjust to a new and different country, when, in fact, they may simply be growing up as all children do. This representation works against the children, who feel the burden to "normalize" their behavior as American. It functions as an obstacle placed before marginalized persons to remind them of their tenuous status.[25]

I heed this critique in this study. By linking consumption and Asian America, I do not contend that children of immigrants (or children of immigrant entrepreneurs in particular) are more consumptive or materially superficial than other ethnic groups. Instead, I argue that second generation Chinese Americans and Korean Americans who grew up in small family businesses function as strategically insightful groups that illustrate the meaning of consumption that is distinctive to their current position within the U.S. political economy. And, as Holt and Schor note in their revisiting of Veblen's classic 1899 theory of the leisure class: "Central to Veblen's analyses were the ideas that consuming is a means of social communication; that it communicates class and income differences."[26] I would also contend that how one consumes communicates political allegiance, particularly for those who straddle the marginal line between "patriotism" and "betrayal."[27] Subsequently, the experiences of children of immigrants are important sources of information in the continued pursuit of greater comprehension of American identity.

Children of Chinese and Korean Immigrants: Growing Up Asian American

The social process of Asian American identity and community construction is the topic of much discussion in both popular and scholarly circles. Beyond individual curiosity, this interest functions as a litmus test of the strength of the social contract, or of the expectations that constitute the national U.S. identity. The process of inclusion and exclusion of particular groups is a telling indicator of what ideologies and principles compose the core of what is or is not "America."

For most Korean and Chinese immigrants, understanding what it means to be *Asian* begins upon arrival to the United States. Prior to migration, their identity was unquestionably that of the national majority.[28] Many immigrants and subsequent generations find "Asia" to be a largely Western construction that combines numerous distinct countries that happen to reside in relative global proximity. For the second generation, this Asian American identity is important in establishing one's legitimate presence in the United States by evoking a communal ethnic history and a sense of a larger collective community. The fact that second generation Korean and Chinese Americans respond so similarly to questions about their lives, despite their seemingly vast cultural differences, is understandable within this logic. The disciplinary power to "fit in" is clear. What remains unclear are what the children experience in achieving this apparent adaptation and what these experiences imply about who we are as a country.

Two of the most apparent differences between Korean Americans and Chinese Americans are in the respective size of each group's first migration wave and in the diversity within the second migration wave. While the Chinese constituted the largest presence within the first Asian migration, there were relatively few Koreans prior to 1965.[29] Consequently, today's Chinese Americans reflect greater generational diversity, which stretches from the first to the fifth generation. The second major difference between the Chinese and Korean migration to the United States is the regional variation within each migration wave. Early Chinese immigration originated almost entirely in five small regions in the southern provinces of Fujian, Guangdong, and the island of Hainan, reflecting the limited economic and military reach of the United States during the first wave. Post-1965, Chinese immigrants have come from a number of different regions, including Hong Kong, Taiwan, mainland China, as well as Vietnam and Singapore.[30] As a result, the second wave of Chinese migration includes different languages, identities, political ideologies, and social classes. Today, a Chinese American's social class is often tied to his or her place of origin and date of migration. For instance, Taiwanese immigrants who arrived in the 1970s came with student visas and acquired high levels of education and skills. Then, in 1979, the Taiwanese government did away with restrictions on overseas travel and a new wave of immigrants came with tourist visas. These later immigrants, along with the family members sponsored by the earlier student migrants, came from more diverse educational and socioeconomic backgrounds.[31] Some of the more recent arrivals have been poor, undocumented wage laborers from mainland China, along with professionals and capitalists from Hong Kong in the years leading up to the 1997 handover. This wide social bifurcation within the Chinese community in the United States has been characterized as the "Uptown" versus "Downtown" Chinese.[32] Subsequently, ethnic solidarity among Chinese immigrants appears to form along linguistic, national, regional, and socioeconomic lines.

On the other hand, Korean immigrants have all migrated from South Korea and share the same language and national identity.[33] The changes in U.S. immigration policy coincided with South Korea's entrance into the world economy, creating the impetus for migration.[34] Pyong Gap Min notes that upon arrival, most Korean immigrants join a Korean church and participate in at least one Korean association, furthering their ethnic immigrant solidarity.[35] The Korean immigrant community is almost entirely a recent phenomenon (post-1965). Not only were there few Korean immigrants during the first wave of Asian migration, homeland politics completely drained the limited resources of Koreans in the United States. The nationalist struggle for independence from U.S. occupation hindered their capital accumulation in the United States, thus restricting the development of an ethnic enclave to function as a central channel for upward socioeconomic mobility, as it had among Chinese and Japanese immigrants at that time.[36] Sucheng Chan writes, "With virtually every avenue of access to the larger society blocked, their fierce involvement in the Korean independence struggle was at once a cause and a result of the circumstances under which they lived."[37] Then, from the 1970s through 1988 was the height of Korean migration to the United States. Most of these individuals came with professional skills and white-collar backgrounds. According to In-Jin Yoon, the number began to increase and the socioeconomic composition of Korean immigrants began to change in 1988, when South Korea successfully hosted the Olympic Games in Seoul.[38] This international event highlighted the heightened social status and economic success of South Korea in a time of deepening U.S. economic recession. Since then, there has been a decline in the number of new arrivals from Korea, and more of these arrivals are from the working class. Yoon points out that, recently, economic advancement in South Korea has not been evenly distributed.[39]

TABLE 2.1

*Perceptions of Parental Priorities by Ethnicity**

Priorities	Chinese American (n=35)	Korean American (n=36)
Children		
Children, in general	9	11
Children's education	9	12
Children & business	1	2
Children & God	3	3
Subtotal	22 (67%)	28 (78%)
Family		
Family, in general	2	0
Family's economic security	5	1
Family's happiness	2	2
Family's health	0	1
Subtotal	9 (27%)	4 (11%)
Other		
Business	2	0
Money	2	1
God	0	1
Self	0	1
Don't know	0	1
Subtotal	4 (11%)	4 (11%)

* Respondents were asked, "What is your parents' number one priority in life?"

Those with modest incomes have experienced a growing sense of relative deprivation and they are utilizing migration as a strategy for upward mobility.

Surprisingly, these significant cultural and historical variations result in relatively few differences in responses among the current population of second generation Chinese and Korean Americans.[40] It was apparent in the interview discussions regarding their work and family life that for both

TABLE 2.2

Language Spoken at Home by Ethnicity

	Chinese	Chinese& English	Korean	Korean& English	English
Entrepreneurial Children					
Chinese Am. (n=35)	6 (17%)	26 (74%)	0	0	3 (8%)
Korean Am. (n=36)	0	0	5 (14%)	29 (81%)	2 (6%)
Non-entrepreneurial Children					
Chinese Am. (n=10)	1 (10%)	9 (90%)	0	0	0
Korean Am. (n=7)	0	0	1 (14%)	6 (86%)	0

groups, their shared experience as children of *Asian* immigrants eclipsed the stark differences in their respective backgrounds. Their collective identity as an *Asian American* is solidified early in childhood and is deeply embedded in their familial roles. In conversations about their role in the family, the respondents repeatedly highlight the importance of their family as culturally "Asian." In fact, "Asia" is ideologically constructed through family processes. For instance, regardless of their ethnic differences, both Korean American and Chinese American second generation young adults are very clear about their roles and expectations within the familial construction. When asked, "What is your parents' number one priority in life?" (see Table 2.1), 94 percent of Chinese Americans and 89 percent of Korean Americans in the sample stated that children and/or family are their parents' first priority. They explained that this was an "Asian" trait.

More specifically, children's education ranked very high in their responses, and was also designated as part of being "Asian." The four Chinese American and four Korean American respondents who report other parental priorities (that do not include themselves) expressed varying degrees of dissatisfaction with their relationship with their parents. Apparently, while parental priorities that stress children may produce a burdensome sense of obligation among the children, they also help maintain a relatively close (sometimes too close) familial connection. Those who do not feel the stress of high parental expectations report feeling distant from one or both of their parents. They understand "Asian" families to center around the children, which can be both good and bad for the child.

Korean Americans and Chinese Americans also report similar patterns in what languages are spoken at home. Given the frequent role of the second generation as translator, the language spoken at home can determine what kinds of expectations the children experience. Also, using languages (other than English) significantly marks the family as foreign/other and thereby requires further ideological negotiation by the child.

The majority in both ethnic groups grew up in bilingual homes, with 74 percent of Chinese Americans and 81 percent of Korean Americans stating that a mixture of their respective ethnic language and English was spoken at home. Only three of the 35 Chinese Americans and two of the 36 Korean Americans spoke only English at home. Aside from these five respondents, all the others interviewed for this study were bilingual to some degree. Both the entrepreneurial and the non-entrepreneurial sample show similarly high rates of bilingualism. To varying degrees, the children of immigrants in both entrepreneurial and non-entrepreneurial families perform translation duties (as discussed further in Chapter Three) as required. However, added expectations come with this ability within entrepreneurial settings. Many times in entrepreneurial families, the children's language ability becomes necessary as part of the business. This breaching of boundaries between home and work appears to produce a greater sense of burden for the children. This was evident in the respondents' discussion of the reasons why they work and whether or not they found the work stressful, for example. While both entrepreneurial and non-entrepreneurial children report high rates of employment, all but one of the entrepreneurial respondents felt some level of obligation to help the family as the primary reason for working. On the other hand, only one non-entrepreneurial respondent stated that he / she was working to help out the family. In addition, 76 percent (54 out of 71) of entrepreneurial children found their work stressful, but only 35 percent (6 out of 17) of non-entrepreneurial children did. This stark difference exists despite the fact that in both categories, children performed similar duties at their place of employment. The particular duties did not induce this stress; rather it is the familial context of the place in which the duties are performed. The meaning and weight of their role

TABLE 2.3
Entrepreneurial Parents' Education
by Ethnicity and Gender

	Jr. High	HS/ Some HS	College/ Some coll.	Grad./Prof. School	D/N
Chinese American (n=70)					
Father (n=35)	1 (3%)	14 (40%)	9 (26%)	9 (26%)	2 (6%)
Mother (n=35)	0	19 (54%)	7 (20%)	8 (23%)	1 (3%)
Subtotal	1 (1%)	33 (47%)	16 (23%)	17 (24%)	3 (4%)
Korean American (n=72)					
Father (n=36)	1 (3%)	9 (25%)	19 (53%)	6 (17%)	1 (3%)
Mother (n=36)	1 (3%)	11 (31%)	21 (58%)	3 (8%)	0
Subtotal	2 (3%)	20 28%)	40 (56%)	9 (13%)	1 (1%)

become heavier as children of entrepreneurial households perform double duty, as worker *and* family member.

The Asian Immigrant Enterprise

According to the children of immigrant entrepreneurs, the reason why their parents own a small family business is for them, and more specifically, their education. This is, in fact, not far from the truth. As stated earlier, self-employment by Korean immigrants is largely a form of underemployment. The educational backgrounds of the respondents' parents in this study tell an interesting story of the meaning of education for immigrants. In my sample, 47 percent of Chinese immigrant parents and 69 percent of Korean immigrant parents have some college education or more. Of these parents, 24 percent of the Chinese and 13 percent of the Korean sample hold professional or graduate degrees. The education levels of fathers and mothers are comparable. However, another 48 percent of Chinese immigrants and 31 percent of Korean immigrants have a high school degree or less. These numbers indicate some bifurcation in education levels and

TABLE 2.4

Entrepreneurial Household Income/Class
by Ethnicity (Self-reported)*

	Working Class (>$30,000)	Middle Class ($30,000- 69,999)	Upper Class ($70,000- 300,000)	D/N
Chinese Am. (n=35)	2 (6%)	20 (57%)	12 (34%)	1 (3%)
Korean Am. (n=36)	2 (6%)	29 (81%)	4 (11%)	1 (3%)
Total (n=71)	4 (6%)	49 (69%)	16 (23%)	2 (3%)

* These household income numbers and class designations are estimates provided by the respondents. These numbers may or may not reflect the actual household income. Respondents were asked to provide both a numerical response and a class designation. Some were reluctant to provide a class designation. In these circumstances, the author of this study classified their numerical responses accordingly (lower, middle, or upper).

class status of immigrants prior to migration.[41] Interestingly, the sense of upward mobility for those families with modest origins is tempered by the overwhelming feeling that the immigrant entrepreneur holds a relatively lowly social position, given the vast amount of time and energy expended. The parents' investment of both educational background and backbreaking manual/service labor appears to have an insufficient return, from the perspective of children who watch their exhausted parents. At the same time, both parents and children understand this significant downward mobility in social status as a temporary slump of the immigrant generation. The second generation, through education made possible by parental sacrifice, is expected to go beyond the first. Therefore, education is understood not as a philosophical luxury, but as a practical means towards an end. It is the repayment of familial obligations to which the second generation so consistently refers. This repayment goes beyond monetary compensation. Instead, it is the social status that education can buy that is crucial here. In this way, education is "conspicuously consumed" to lift their modest social position.

It is helpful to look at the household income and/or class self-reported by children of immigrants in order to comprehend their understanding of this social position.

TABLE 2.5

Household Income Distribution by Race, 1999

	API	White	Black	Am. Indian
Under 25,000	24	29	45	43
$25,000–94,999	53	56	48	51
$95,000 and over	23	15	7	6

SOURCE: U.S. Department of Commerce, Bureau of the Census, Current Population Survey, March Supplement 2000.

In strictly economic terms, the family enterprise can provide a decent standard of living (for those 50 percent whose business does not fail). Both Korean Americans and Chinese Americans in this study most often designate themselves as middle-class (Korean Americans more so than Chinese Americans, 81 percent versus 57 percent). These numbers may or may not reflect the actual household income, given the variation in the children's knowledge of the family's finances. Instead, these estimates are more insightful in understanding how the respondents perceive their place within the larger U.S. social hierarchy. Likewise, most respondents view themselves as within the economic "norm" of U.S. society. This economic indicator is perceived as a crucial step towards the goal of greater social acceptance.

There are some distinctions, however. The Chinese American respondents report a more even distribution among the three class categories. Korean Americans in this study have higher parental education levels on average than Chinese Americans, but report a lower income level. These data are in line with the 1990 census, which shows the overall socioeconomic profile of Chinese Americans as higher than that of Korean Americans.[42] Economic returns on parental education appear more modest for Korean Americans, perhaps dampening the rags-to-riches narrative for Korean immigrants. This may, in turn, place greater pressure on second generation Korean Americans to reverse the wage and social status decline their parents experienced.

According to aggregate census data, the majority of Asian/Pacific Islanders (API) in the United States also describe themselves as middle-class.

TABLE 2.6

Business Density Among API-Owned Firms, 1997

Racial/Ethnic Group	Number of Firms	Percent[1]	Business Density[2]
All U.S. Firms	20,821,934	100	13.5
Nonminority	17,782,901	85.40	n/a
All Minority	3,039,033	14.60	n/a
All Asian/Pacific Islander	912,929	4.38	11.7
Asian Indian	166,737	18.26	10.1
Chinese	252,577	27.67	9.6
Filipino	84,534	9.26	21.9
Japanese	85,538	9.37	9.3
Korean	135,571	14.85	7.9
Vietnamese	97,764	10.71	11.5
Other Asian	70,868	7.76	18.1
Hawaiian	15,544	1.70	9.0
Other Pacific Islander	3,826	0.42	67.5

[1] Percentages for first four lines are a share of total U.S. firms; percentages for Asian subgroups are a share of Asian-owned businesses.
[2] Business density is defined as the number of individuals in the population (2000) per firm owned by a member of the population (1997). The different years of population and firm data will create some distortion in this approximate figure.
SOURCE: U.S. Department of Commerce, Bureau of the Census, SMOBE, 1997.

It is worthy of mention that, in fact, most whites, Blacks, and American Indians are classified as middle-class as well. However, African Americans and Native Americans had larger shares of their respective population at lower income levels. Within the Asian/Pacific Islander population, as many families live in poverty as live in affluence. The substantial economic division of this population is very clear.

Overall, Asian/Pacific Islanders comprise a disproportionate number of entrepreneurs in the United States. Census numbers show that APIs were 3.6 percent of the total U.S. population and 12.3 percent of the total minority population in 2000. However, they owned 4.4 percent of all U.S. business firms and 30 percent of all minority-owned firms in 1997. Business

TABLE 2.7

Top Industry Receipt Leaders for API-Owned Firms, 1997

Industry	Receipts		
	All API ($ Million)	Chinese ($1,000)	Korean ($1,000)
Wholesale Trade	105,466		
Wholesale trade—durable goods	64,884	34,065	7,462
Wholesale trade—nondurable goods	40,585	18,621	5,884
Retail Trade	67,895		
Food stores	17,247	3,217	5,718
Eating and drinking places	15,804	8,484	1,751
Automotive dealers and service stations	14,213	1,468	4,341
Services	67,762		
Health services	22,358	3,735	1,486
Business services	14,732	4,071	2,897
Engineering and management services	10,876	3,273	1,357

SOURCE: U.S. Department of Commerce, Bureau of the Census, SMOBE, 1997.

density rates—which measure the number of individuals in the population divided by the number of businesses in the population (the lower the number, the higher the business density)—show that API businesses averaged 11.7 points, higher than the national average of 13.5. Table 2.6 gives the breakdown by specific API ethnicities.

Among the API population, Korean Americans have the highest business density, at 7.9. Chinese Americans also have relatively high rates of self-employment, higher than both the API and national averages. Filipinos are remarkable in their low rate of entrepreneurialism. Their greater English-language proficiency, as a result of their unique history with the United States, may provide other avenues for employment.

Of these firms, most are very small. According to a report by the U.S. Small Business Administration (SBA), this is the case for most U.S. firms; only 25.4 percent of all U.S. firms had paid employees in 1997.[43] Approximately 31 percent of Asian American-owned firms had paid employees, and on average, these firms employed no more than seven people. To get a better sense of the variety of API businesses, Table 2.7 shows sales receipts by industry.

API-owned enterprises are heavily concentrated in three industries: wholesale trade, retail trade, and services. After wholesale trade, retail trade in food stores brought in the highest sales receipts for Korean Americans; for Chinese Americans, eating and drinking establishments brought in the highest sales receipts in 1997. The majority of the respondents in this study were involved in retail trade. The average receipt per API-owned firm was $336,200, lower than the $410,000 average for all U.S. firms.[44] However, 28 percent of API firms reported receipts of less than $10,000 in 1997 while 5 percent of API firms reported sales of $1 million or more.[45] There are apparently significant differences in sales receipts within each industry. Those enterprises with low receipts are most prone to business failure. However, failure is in no way limited to only these 28 percent, given the reality that approximately half of all small businesses started in the U.S. will fail. The SBA's Office of Advocacy examined minority business turnover using a database of firms with employees and found that 50.4 percent of API businesses that started in 1992 survived for at least four years.[46] This survival rate is actually slightly higher than the national average of 47 percent. This may be a consequence of API's concentration in service industries, which have the highest survival rates among minority-owned businesses, because entry costs tend to be lower than in goods-producing industries. There are also stark differences in business survival rates by race. For instance, the highest survival rate was almost 82 percent, for non-Hispanic white-owned businesses in the capital-intensive oil and gas extraction industry. Even the fifth highest survival rate, for non-Hispanic white businesses, was near 70 percent.[47]

The SBA report cites lack of financial capital as one of the many impediments to the survival of small firms, and minority-owned firms in particular. In his study of Korean immigrant entrepreneurs in Chicago and Los Angeles, Yoon found that capital was accumulated through multiple sources, including personal savings in the United States, loans from family and friends, and Korean-style rotating credit associations called *kyes*.[48] All these sources are internal in the ethnic community and facilitate the development of business credit when loans from more formal financial institu-

TABLE 2.8

*States with the Largest Number of Asian- and Pacific
Islander–Owned Firms*

State	Number of API-owned firms
California	316,048
New York	123,258
Texas	60,226
Hawaii	50,634
New Jersey	41,432
Illinois	36,857
Florida	33,769
Washington	23,309
Virginia	22,441
Maryland	22,164

SOURCE: U.S. Department of Commerce, Bureau of the Census, SMOBE, 1997.

tions such as banks may be inaccessible. Initial capital accumulation, which is crucial for business survival, requires an effective utilization of class, family, and ethnic resources. Ivan Light and others also note that many immigrant entrepreneurs acquire their initial business training in the course of an apprenticeship undertaken in the business of a coethnic.[49] Given the need for these embedded social networks within ethnic communities, it is not surprising to find greater numbers of API-owned firms in areas with large API populations.

According to census figures, nearly six out of ten minority-owned firms were in just five states. California, Texas, New York, Florida, and Illinois accounted for 59 percent of the nation's minority-owned firms. California had the largest number of minority-own firms (including API-owned firms) with 738,000, but Hawaii had the highest proportion, with 58 percent.[50] The regional distribution of entrepreneurial respondents in this study falls largely within these expectations, with 70 percent from California (n = 24) and Illinois (n = 26). Most of the children of immigrants interviewed for this study grew up with strong connections to their ethnic community. It is reasonable to assume that those raised in predominantly white communities experienced greater degrees of marginalization than those in Asian-centered communities,[51] but this was not necessarily the case for everyone in this particular study. Ethnic community effects were not so clear-cut. For instance, a young Chinese American man growing up in Lawrence, Kansas, exhibited a strong sense of his ethnic identity, which seemed to derive from an extremely small but tight-knit local ethnic community. At the same time, another young Chinese American from Orange County, California, which has a large Asian American population, spoke at length about his sense of alienation from his own ethnic community. It seems that ethnic community networks can be too strong as well as not strong enough regardless of community size.

Immigrant Self-Discipline

In-Jin Yoon writes: "Immigrant life consists of constant doubt and justification of one's reasons for being in a foreign land."[52] This simple statement goes to the core of the immigrant experience. What is clear from speaking with the children of these immigrants is that this doubt does not end with the immigrant generation. For the second generation, their life consists of constant doubt and justification of their reasons for being in, not a foreign land, but their *own* land. Legal documentation of citizenship has little to do with a social sense of belonging—it is only the beginning. As Nazli Kibria notes: "[Asian Americans] lack acceptance in the dominant society, *in conjunction with and despite their involvement and participation in it.*"[53] This is a crucial point that alludes to Espiritu's notion of differential inclusion. The issue is not about whether the individual is adapting (i.e., performing the "right" behavior towards the goal of "productive" economic independence) properly but rather the ways in which children of immigrants are disciplined into a particular place within the larger social hierarchy. The stories of entrepreneurial children extend the argument that Asian Americans are made to exemplify a specific national narrative of meritocracy and capitalism in which conspicuous consumption leads to greater social citizenship. According to this national ideology, the ideal citizenship status for Asian Americans is one of self-discipline (i.e., the "Good Immigrant")—an unquestioned acceptance and perpetuation of social inequality. The interviews documented in this book disrupt this notion by providing greater depth on the children's everyday experiences of growing up a perpetual foreigner in one's own land.

In the next chapter I delve into the significance of the social construction of the "normal" American family in the lives of second generation Asian Americans. Here, I argue that the pursuit of this ideological construct requires the containment of one's difference. Consumption becomes an essential strategy of containment as an expression of one's "normality" for those who find themselves in such seemingly "abnormal" circumstances as that of a demanding small family business.

CHAPTER THREE

Searching for a "Normal" Family

You know that stupid show that comes on Fridays? You know, the one with the perfect white kids and the twins? I think it's called *Full House*. Well, I *hate* that show. All those stupid kids with their stupid problems—"oh no, my outfit doesn't match and my hair's messed up!" And I *hate* the parents too. It's so unrealistic. I mean do the parents work or what?! They're always at home with the kids trying to solve their stupid problems!
—Michelle, 16, Chinese American

In addressing the question of *why* Asian Americans are made to prove their social citizenship, this chapter explores the family as a site of difference that marks the experiences of Asian Americans as marginal. The ideology of the "American family" has played a powerful role in U.S. culture. This ode to white, middle-class, heterosexual, nuclear families has repeatedly been raised as the core of our social values,[1] and, not coincidentally, it is also the fundamental unit of consumption.[2] In describing a new "commodity frontier" in the United States, Arlie Russell Hochschild notes that increasing declines in private and public resources for intimate/domestic care, in conjunction with increasing demands for longer work hours, have transformed the family from a unit of production to one of consumption.[3] This phenomenon is nothing new for immigrant entrepreneurial families. Family business households are commodified environments that require both producers and consumers. Limited familial resources coupled with an intense workplace labor demand are an everyday experience, and one that children of these families understand intimately. Children of immigrants must take on multiple roles to fulfill the daily needs of not only the family, but also the family business. The family, many times, functions to meet the demands of consumers. And, although they may not have the purchasing power to overcome these market demands (i.e., pay someone else to perform the tasks), these second generation Asian Americans employ consumptive fantasies to imagine a "normal" American family. These consumptive fantasies motivate second generation Asian Americans to behave in certain ways that befit the ideal American family.

This chapter focuses on the rationale behind consumption (and consumption fantasies) for Korean and Chinese American children of immigrant entrepreneurs. I argue that the discomfort or disjuncture that these children experience as part of an ethnic immigrant entrepreneurial family is "contained" or lessened through consumption. Posed against the formidable and largely fictive "American family" ideal, the real familial experiences and relationships appear different, and consequently negative. This chapter will show how these young adults and adolescents deal with the work and family constraints they face.

Containing Difference

In a study of Korean and Vietnamese American college students, Karen Pyke found that the "normal American family" was used as an interpretive framework to make sense of their family life.[4] Likewise, the respondents in this study presented starkly dichotomous images of what they understood to be American (emotionally open and lenient, but individualistic) versus Asian (emotionally distant and strict, but collective) families. Pyke convincingly argues that the American family, as a normative moral dogma, shapes the consciousness and perspective of those whom it excludes.[5] In this way, the normal American family functions to marginalize those deemed as "others." The question, then, is how do Asian America children (as members of an "othered" group) interpret and confront this ideology?

One, and perhaps the most rational, possibility is to reject one and accept the other (American versus Asian). However, the immigrant family is a complicated terrain and such simplistic solutions are not realistic. Children growing up in this environment—particularly those in entrepreneurial settings—must negotiate a variety of roles, obligations, and expectations. I would argue that *both* the American and the Asian images of family are controlling ideologies that the children of Asian immigrants construct and maintain as a way to "normalize" differences. The differences are "contained" in a way that not only leaves undisturbed the ideology of the *American* family but also reinforces it with the *Asian* family to create an "Asian American" family.

For those in small family businesses, this containment of difference is useful because multiple and contradictory responsibilities require these Asian Americans to function as both worker (i.e., adult) and family member (i.e., child). The necessity for a mental process, or "boundary work,"[6] to separate home and work, coupled with conflicting family role expectations, makes the family business especially complicated. The social context of the immigrant small business creates an environment that requires children who grow up within it to adhere to unique developmental expectations (this is discussed in greater detail in Chapter Four). For these adolescents and young adults, the embedded nature of work and home in the context of Asian immigrant small businesses does not allow for the customary rites of passage during their teenage years. Successful boundary work is important for the second generation—this process is necessary to make a connection and "normalize" their relationship with their parents. Boundary work is a way to bring together two seemingly opposite or contradictory concerns and minimize the differences that separate the two without fundamentally altering either. It is a delicate negotiation—and one that facilitates consumption. Once again, difference is consumed as the "Asian" otherness is contained in a neat box that fits nicely within the larger "American" context.

This chapter focuses on the efforts of these young adults to make sense of and "normalize" the differences they perceive in their family. I first examine the ways in which they define and discuss the "American" preoccupation with "quality family time." Second, I address how and why these children describe their mother's and/or father's parenting ability by juxtaposing their experiences against those of the "normal" American family. Third, I illustrate the embedded nature of work and family boundaries in small family businesses and the challenges this poses for successful boundary work. This chapter highlights the family life of children of immigrant entrepreneurs as they negotiate the intrusion of the larger economy and its consumers. Interestingly, these same children harbor consumptive fantasies as a way to overcome these intrusions.

Normalizing Work and Family

Finding Quality Family Time When the
Customer Is Always First

Only sixteen out of the seventy-one (23 percent) respondents inter-viewed for this study stated that they felt they had had enough quality fam-ily time while growing up in an immigrant entrepreneurial household.[7] The definitions of quality time provided by the respondents were remark-ably similar and relatively simple. Chau, a 16-year-old Korean American male said, "Quality family time is pretty much any time we're all together doing nothing, not worrying about anything, sharing our home, eating dinner, talking." Likewise, Sage, a 22-year-old Chinese American female, said, "Quality family time is when we're all together and none of us have any other responsibilities, just hanging out. None of us has any stress that we have to be elsewhere, just enjoying, talking about the past." There is very little variation in the definition—uninterrupted togetherness, com-fort/ ease, and talking/listening.

These definitions indicate a ritualized and sacred sense of family. "Family" is constructed not just of bodies but of what these bodies do in relation to each other at particular times. Therefore, what makes a "time" one of "quality" and "family" is the meaning derived from the social envi-ronment and type of interaction among the family members, that is, relax-ing, being unhurried, and being just among family members—the oppo-site of most family businesses. Tony, a 19-year-old Chinese American, said, "I'd say there's a lot of family coming together because we're always at the store together, but in terms of quality it's not that great." Tony's family owns a smoke shop in Silicon Valley. He added, "My family never vaca-tions. We don't do anything together as a family except work. When we come home, I'll watch TV or read. My dad will read the Chinese newspa-per. My mom will watch TV or chill out. We don't do anything together. We haven't eaten dinner together since the early 1990s." Despite all the hours spent in the same small store, the interaction among the family members is described as lacking in "quality." The value of working hours is diminished by the social context in which it is experienced. The subject matter of discussion is often limited in depth and length because it is understood that they may be interrupted by the ringing of the bell above the door signaling the entrance of another customer.

Family time or quality family time is understood as central to modern family life in the United States.[8] In the recent debate on "family values," lack of time was reported as the biggest perceived threat to American families". Historian John Gillis argues for the importance of understanding the "hidden dimension" of time[9] beyond the overly simplistic notion of family time as universal and unchanging. Gillis writes that " . . . virtually all our family occasions, from the daily dinner to the annual holidays, and including the great life-cycle events like christenings, weddings, and funerals, are the product of the second half of the nineteenth century" that emerged as part of the capitalist industrial society.[10] In today's post-industrial society, these family occasions remain salient in American life and at the same time are more difficult to manage given the increasing work demands.[11] According to Ong and Hee, approximately 42 percent of Asian American business owners work fifty hours or more a week, and 26 percent work sixty hours or more.[12] When asked how long their parents worked at the family business, 87 percent (sixty-two out of seventy-one) of respondents in this study reported that their father worked an average of seventy hours a week and 80 percent reported that their mother worked an average of seventy hours a week.

Interestingly, whether or not a respondent said they had enough quality family time had no correlation with how close they felt to their mother or father. Nor did it make any difference what type of business the family owned. Rather, the lack of quality family time was approached as a fact of life that accompanies their livelihood. As much as they may feel a sense of loss or grief from not having enough quality time to satisfy them, the children view this shortfall as beyond their parents' control and, perhaps even more important, something that is collectively felt by all members of the family. Tony's relationship with his father illustrates this complexity:

> We argue all the time, every day. That hasn't changed since high school. Every day. My dad, he's pretty old. All he cares about is reading the Chinese paper. He keeps all these newspapers around the house, from 1985. It's just crazy. You come in the house and there's a frigging mountain of papers. He'll get pretty pissed off if you tell him to move it to his room or his den, and he won't. He'll buy three papers a day. He doesn't have

time to read them, so he's going to save them. We argue about how messy it is.

At the same time, Tony is very clear that his parents do not embarrass him. He is careful not to speak badly of this father but at the same time is honest in expressing his frustration. Collecting newspapers since 1985, the year they opened their family store, is both crazy and not so crazy, given the circumstances. In a manner akin to Arlie Hochschild's description of corporate office workers who keep mementos of what they would do in the future when they find the time,[13] Tony's father appears adamant about "making up" for all the lost time that he put into the family business. Rather than letting go, he is holding on to another part of his life, determined to catch up when he finally retires. Another respondent, Andrew, described how his family was able to afford luxury items such as a giant television after years of working at the family restaurant, only to never find the time to watch it, given the continued labor demands at the business.

Catching up with time lost, unfortunately, is easier said than done. For instance, as the children grow older, they are finding themselves working as hard as their parents. Sky, a 22-year-old Korean American, explained, "Our lives are still so busy. It used to be that I wanted so much time with my parents. But now, I don't have time for them. We're always missing each other. They're now complaining that we never have time for them. It's turned around." Consequently, it becomes difficult to blame their parents for the absence of quality time together when they themselves are so busy. Jin, a 23-year-old Korean American, is unique in this study, in that his parents are one of only two who are retired. At the time of his interview, his parents had recently sold the family diner: "They've been retired about four months. It's like, let's go fishing, let's go camping. And they want to do that now that they have time. They want to travel. And now we're working our asses off and we don't have time."

Tony, whose family owns the smoke shop, added, "We all understand that that's just the way it is. When we come home at the end of the day, we want to rest before we go to sleep and go to work again. I don't feel like I get enough quality time, but I don't see it as critically important to my development." Tony's matter-of-fact manner typifies the responses of the young adults in this study.

Relationship with Parents: "Don't Ask, Don't Tell"

Sarah, a 20-year-old Chinese American, described her relationship with her parents thus: "We don't clash too much. We're not a very open family. We don't really talk all that much about controversial things. It's like, don't ask, don't tell. Keep it to yourself. We don't really get into it. I'm sure if we really discussed some issues we would have problems." Sarah's parents own a car wash in southern California. Her parents have worked at the business for twenty-one years from 7:00 A.M. to 6:00 P.M. every day, seven days a week (except for one week of vacation a year). Despite the annual vacation, Sarah reports that she does not feel that she has enough quality family time, in the form of dinner and leisurely conversation. Given the scarcity of uninterrupted time together, Sarah chooses to refrain from subject matter that would cause friction. As Li, a 21-year-old Chinese American, told me, "The time we do spend together, why waste it on arguing?"

Similarly, Kirsten, a 20-year-old Chinese American, said, "We love each other very much but we don't talk about very many things." In general, the young adults want to maintain a close relationship with their parents with minimal conflict. Dean, an 18-year-old Korean American, explained:

> [My father] was really strict growing up. I thought he was just an asshole. Now I kind of understand why he did it. My mom would just yell a lot. More than anything else, she used the I'm-very-disappointed-in-you guilt trip approach. But . . . I've never been a parent, so I can't really judge them; for the most part they've been good. I can't complain. I think I turned out pretty well [laughs].

In these families, the children have an underlying and largely unspoken connection with their parents. While this characteristic could be construed as "Korean," given that studies of children in Korea conclude that parental strictness is associated with warmth and concern and that its absence is understood as a sign of neglect,[14] that does not fully explain how Korean American children interpret their relationship with their parents. Asian Americans provide a more complex scenario, in which the "difference" of their immigrant parents' child-raising practices within the peculiar circumstances of the family business are real and deeply felt. They do not automatically or easily interpret strictness as warmth and concern. However, nor do they reject their parents as "bad" parents for not raising them in an idealistically "American" way (i.e., emphasizing sensitivity, open honest communication, flexibility, and forgiveness.[15]) Instead, they use the dichotomous ideological constructions of "Asian" parent (strict, stoic) and "American" parent (flexible, open) in particular ways to render a mostly positive comparison of their parents.

For instance, 20-year-old Bob said this about his father: "He's never hit me in my life, which is a rarity in Korean families. He has always spoken to me very rationally and logically. Instead of beating me with a stick, he's caused me to think about my actions. In that sense it's a very good parenting style." Twenty-one-year-old Korean American Edward said, "Not to be stereotypical, but there is a difference in how males are raised in Korea and the rest of Asia. It's not like you would have the American image of father and son throwing a baseball. I never had that. In a lot of ways, I feel like I haven't interacted with my dad, but in other ways I am close to him." Edward feels a connection with his father that is largely unspoken and subtle. Part of what makes the parental relationship for second generation Asian Americans so complex is the deep linkage between their own ethnic identity and their understanding of their parents. Many times, the parents become the primary conduit for the children to experience "Korean" or "Chinese" culture, which then informs how the children construct their own ethnic identity. Edward knows his father through an indirect understanding of his own identification with what he deems to be "Korean" culture. He went on to say:

> In Korean society people will judge the parents according to the merits of their children. I'm aware of that. So far, because I'm in an Ivy League school and my Korean's very proper, I present myself as a well-mannered person. I'm not trying to be a mascot or a showcase kid, but I know that there are roles that I fulfill that it's not something that you really think about. I became more aware of it as I grew older because once in a while my parents would talk to me and say, "The person we met, they said this and this and they were very impressed about this." or they will tell me, "Your actions reflect upon us." If we see a kid who is very visibly a bad kid, doing things that aren't appropriate or acceptable, they'll say, "Kids like that reflect badly upon their parents."

Other Korean American families play an important instructional role in demonstrating not only how "good" and "bad" children behave, but also how "Korean" or "Asian" the child is. In Edward's case, being "Korean" means a brand-name education, formal Korean language ability, and good manners. There is both subtle and overt pressure on him to conform to cultural ideals, whatever they may be. For those who grew up in communities with very few Asian Americans, this ideal remains steadfast, just as it is for those living in Los Angeles or San Francisco, but conformity requires a specific set of strategies. Sky, the 22-year-old Korean American, grew up in a small town in Illinois and then went away to a small college with very little racial diversity. Her family owns a dry cleaning store. She said:

> All my friends are white. That's just what I know. It's not exactly out of choice. It's just what's in front of me. Whatever I'm exposed to, I'll deal with accordingly. So now my mom's all worried: "She's going to marry a white person! What am I going to do?! How have I raised you?!" I'm like, Mom, you raised me in a predominantly white society. All I know are white people. I relate to them so much better than to Koreans. Why are you so surprised? You enrolled me in all these white schools. How do you expect me to have Korean friends when there are no other Koreans?

The pressure Sky feels vis-à-vis her marriage prospects is part of her mother's effort to replicate a "good" Korean family for her daughter. It is apparent that her mother sees this effort as an important part of her responsibility as a good Korean mother despite the social circumstances.

For those in a large community of co-ethnics (as in Edward's case), the comparisons with other Korean or Chinese American children are not necessarily more relaxed. What is similar in both cases is the significance of other co-ethnics in helping to define one's own ethnic identity. For Sky, this understanding came to her quite suddenly one day as she walked through the halls of her high school. She recounted the incident in this way:

> I grew up thinking I was white. I didn't know. I had never confronted other Asians besides my cousin with whom I played all the time when I was a child, but in high school all my friends were white. I had one friend who was Korean who moved away. I had issues like, one time I was walking down the hallway in high school talking to my friends. I look over at a glass [mirror] and check to see if I'm okay and my hair's in place, and I'm like, "My god, I'm Asian!" I was not expecting to see a Korean face in the

reflection. That was the turning point. I was so shocked. I ran to the counselor's office and said, "I just realized I was Korean." It was so weird and bizarre. I was expecting to see a white person. After that I decided that I need to acknowledge that I am Korean. How does one do that? How does one force themselves to be Korean when they are Korean?

Sky asks a very important question—how does one become Korean when one is already Korean? This question alludes to the fact that one's "Koreanness" is constructed and maintained. Being "white" for Sky was a form of belonging and acceptance that lasted for some time during her earlier childhood—being white was normal. By adolescence, she is confronted with the common question, "Who am I?" But, unlike her white friends, for her the answer to this question requires that she understand a "different" culture that is marginalized as an "other." The children's relationship with their parents is an important part of this process.

Laura, another Korean American, explained, "I'm still trying to learn not to take things for granted. I've learned the importance of Korean culture. When I think about the dynamics of my relationship with my parents and I see my other friends who aren't Korean and their dynamics, it's different, it's interesting." Of course, not every learning experience is positive. Laura continued, "There are certain dynamics between Korean adults that I don't really like. In Korean culture, adults can say things that I find kind of offensive. It's like, Korean culture allows it. Sometimes some of those offensive remarks are directed towards me." Learning what it means to be "Korean" from one's parents can be a tricky endeavor. The children find themselves having to ascribe particular traits either as "Korean culture" or as one's individual personality—a feat that is especially difficult when parents fall short of their expectations.

To simply declare their parents' child-raising skills to be "bad" is, to some extent, an act of self-denial—denial of one's own ethnic identity. Korean/Chinese culture is intricately tied to how one "parents." Even Victor, a 20-year-old Korean American male, whose parents could be described as stereotypically or negatively "Asian," was careful to present his parents in a particular manner that denoted his respect and gratitude towards them:

My dad is pretty strict. He had to juggle so many things at once. He had four kids, his business—a big thing for him—he's a workaholic. He would be gone most of the day and come home and be stressed out. He'd deal with us the way he could. . . . My mom was kind of strict too. She wanted to be a loving mother, but she could only do so much.

The absence of communication with his parents is not relayed as a deficiency or neglect, but rather as a matter of circumstance. And, in this regard, the business plays a convenient or useful role as the culprit for the loss that Victor feels. This was also evident in Jane's description of her parents, who had recently retired:

I missed out on more family time, vacations, more family anything. I know that my brother definitely resents this—totally—not being able to go to his Boy Scout camping things. It's always the reason for not being able to go. There's something to do with the business. Always. Never anything else. I don't even think they had friends until a few years ago, because of the store.

While the sense of loss is sincere and particularly painful for Jane's younger brother, Jane's family views the business as a source of significant sacrifice for every family member, including the parents. This, then, adds to the complexity of the meaning and role of the business in family life, particularly given the blurring of boundaries between the two sites.

The Embeddedness of Work and Family

The Absence of Boundaries

As Maria, a 20-year-old Chinese American whose family owns a small Chinese take-out, explained, "It's all connected. It's your livelihood. You can't separate it [work] from your home life because your home life depends on it." Maria has played an integral role in her family's business since she was 7 years old, when she began to pack carry-out orders.[16] She had never had a babysitter, and instead remembers a rather pleasant childhood at the restaurant. One of her earliest memories is of playing with paper dolls of Chinese soap opera characters with her older sister. She also recalls her father teaching her and her sister how to play tennis, badminton, and softball behind the store during slow periods of the day.

Kyung Ah, a second generation Korean American, also performs integral labor at her family's jewelry store. She began selling jewelry and watches at the age of 11. However, unlike Maria, Kyung Ah's childhood memories are filled with concern over her parents' safety. After experiencing a number of what she described as "traumatic" robbery attempts at a young age, she continually worries about her parents. Kyung Ah's sense of protectiveness towards her parents pervades both home and work. She said, "It kind of got to where I was treating them like children. . . . I had to remind myself that they're still my parents and they can take care of themselves. They're very resourceful."[17] And when asked if she behaved at the business as she would at home, she replied: "It feels exactly the same, pretty much. Just different surroundings. Instead of being at home, we're at the store. We had a TV, we had a refrigerator, and we always had Korean food for lunch." What contributed to the general trauma of a robbery for Kyung Ah was that the crime took place at the *family* store. It was as if her home were invaded.

However, there are degrees of embeddedness. The small, "mom-and-pop" enterprises in the sample displayed almost no boundaries, but the larger businesses with more than five non-family employees identified specific differences between home and work (see Appendix A for the list of businesses). Robert, a Korean American college senior, whose family owns two small jewelry stores, illustrated this phenomenon. His mother runs the smaller store with one occasional, part-time employee. His mother's store has been losing money for quite some time and is a source of financial concern for the family. His father runs the larger, more profitable store with four employees. Robert discussed how he and his parents interacted at home and at the business:

> I think it's very similar. There's no change whatsoever. I remember my friend, Peter, mentioned that he and his family act a little more professional [at work] but I think that might be a consequence of the kind of business that he's in (an export/import company) and the fact that his father is more of a businessman. He's an MBA, or whatever else. Ours is a very mom and pop kind of thing and so I don't think that anything changes at all.

Robert makes a distinction between his friend's father and his own. Peter's father has a dual role of father at home and businessman at work. However, Robert's father is a father at home and at work. There is no differentiation.

To stress his point, Robert describes what happens when he or his sisters have disagreements with their parents:

> It's played out wherever because of the nature of my parents. They're very impulsive. They're very worried. They can't sit on something and say, "Hum. Well, Robert, we'll talk about it later." It has to come out wherever—the grocery store, wherever. It's just the way they are. . . . The store wasn't any sort of, you know, you don't have to act a certain way at the store. It was the second home, pretty much. And in a sense it felt that way. There was a bed in the back and a TV in the back.

Robert's passage reveals an interesting phenomenon wherein one's family role remains constant despite the circumstances. Robert's father remains his father despite the fact that Robert performs a great deal of the "adult" responsibilities at the family's jewelry store. And, as long as Robert's father remains in the role of the father, Robert remains in the role of the son at home *and work*, no matter how old he becomes. This was also the case with all the other respondents whose family own small mom-and-pop enterprises.

This interweaving of work and home, and adult- and child-status is evident in the way the children are rewarded for their labor. Most are not paid. Robert explained, "I wasn't paid in the normal sense. I got room, board, allowance, and tuition." Rather than a paycheck, the children are given allowances—any money exchanged represents a gift from the parents, not compensation for any particular deed. I asked Maria if she was paid for working at the restaurant. She said: "Yes. I think it started off at five dollars an hour. Or was it four dollars? I don't remember. I don't ever think about it. It's always, 'Thanks, Mom.' It's a gift or something. I didn't care if my parents paid me. I didn't really need it. If I needed something, they'd get it for me." In this way, the work children perform is classified as a household chore, despite the fact that the labor took place within the business. The business is an extension of the home, and the children remain children rather than employees, no matter what their job description.

William, a 20-year-old Korean American, described how he felt about not being paid: "My parents made up for it by giving me spending money when I needed it." In some respects, the parents retain their authority and control over their children's lives by forcing them to make specific requests for money rather than giving it to them automatically. However, the blurred boundaries between work and home make accepting money from parents difficult. Judy made an interesting differentiation between "family" money and "real" money:

> It was really hard for me to tell my parents freshman year that I was going to get a real job and get paid. They said, "We'll pay you," but to me that's not the same thing because they are struggling and for them to give me money—it's like the same family money and I felt like I needed to go out and make separate money to support myself. That was hard, but I think it was a compromise that we both had to make.

That summer, Judy worked at McDonald's deep-frying french fries and thoroughly enjoyed it. The pay was terrible but she felt the money was truly her own. She added that the money came "worry-free," since the work was a "no-brainer." Judy explained to me that working at an outside job gave her a sense of autonomy that she enjoyed for the first time. In addition, she said she felt more like an adult, despite the fact that she performed more adult-like roles at the family business.

Only two of the families I interviewed had the luxury to shield their children from the everyday duties of the business. One was Charlie, a 20-year-old Korean American. His family owns a general merchandise store. I asked why he and his brothers never worked at the store. He said:

> I guess my brothers and I could have worked at the store during the week-ends and vacations, but my parents wanted us to have "normal" lives and not have to worry about working or supporting the family. I think that my parents would have felt that they failed in some sense if the situation required their children working at the store. My parents weren't trying to "protect" us from their store or anything. They just felt that children should just have fun and study.

Charlie's situation is unusual. He explains his good fortune in living a "normal" life as a result of his parent's hard work. His parents work ten- to fourteen-hour days, seven days a week, and have never had a vacation since buying the store in 1982. Apparently, Charlie's "normal" life is a result of his parent's ability to separate work and home for their children. Interestingly, he is somewhat defensive about his lack of involvement in the business, while at the same time, he presents his parents as perhaps more devoted than other parents who expect their children to work.

Charlie's choice of pronouns is also unusual. Throughout the interview, he referred to the family business as "theirs" rather than "ours." Other children with greater personal involvement described the family business as "ours." Charlie's marginal involvement is also indicated in his description of the store. For instance, rather than using familial terms, he uses business terms to describe what his parents do at the store: "Being self-employed offers more freedom, and allows my parents to plow their earnings back into the business and invest in themselves more, i.e., my parents can employ less employees by working harder and longer." Charlie's definition of freedom differs significantly from that of respondents who work at the business on a daily basis. Others saw working harder and longer without the help of employees as difficult but necessary labor, rather than a "freedom."

In Charlie's case, his parents made the conscious decision to hire seasonal employees rather than require unpaid labor from their three sons, despite the fact that doing so resulted in less profit for the family as a whole. However, additional paid employees are not a financial option for most immigrant entrepreneurial families, no matter how hard the parents work.

Implications of Incomplete Boundary Work

Almost all of my interviewees in mom-and-pop businesses described feeling resentment or frustration while working at the family business during their high school years (just one respondent provided only "happy" stories). My interviews with adolescents (and some young adults) who were currently immersed in the work and family paradox were frequently punctuated by emotionally charged responses that revealed anger, sadness, and frustration. For instance, Jenny, a 15-year-old Chinese American student, described her work experience in this way: "It sucks, major!" When probed further, she raised her voice and added:

> I have to work all the time. I don't have time for friends, or to hang out, or just be bored. I have to go to the restaurant after school where I cut the vegetables, wash the dishes, and sweep the floor. Then I have to take care of my younger brothers, clean up the house and try to find time for homework. It's crazy! I hate it! I'm so tired all the time.

Jenny literally rose from her chair during this discussion, making the level of her frustration clear. Such strong emotions were also present in interviews with young men. During my second interview with Robert, silent tears clouded his vision as he described his overwhelming feeling of guilt and obligation to his parents. He, like a number of his peers, had to pause and walk around the room to compose himself. Several male respondents told me: "Sometimes, I just can't breathe."

In general, I found that this claustrophobic feeling among respondents dissipates somewhat with time and distance (sometimes physical, sometimes mental or emotional) from parents and the business. They feel the need to develop their own identity apart from the family and the business. Many respondents achieve this aim through gaining acceptance at a university away from home, creating physical and social distance away from their parents. Afterwards, what remains is a deep-seated protectiveness towards their parents. Jack, a Chinese American college junior, recalled some of the good times he had growing up at his family's Chinese restaurant: "When we were little, we were known as the Fu Shou kids. The restaurant is called Fu Shou. We would create hell. [Laughs.] I remember that. We were basically let loose. My brothers and I were known for being really close." As Jack grew older and more mature, the restaurant also changed to accommodate different functions. For Jack and others, the business became a place to meet friends during their adolescent years. In Jack's case, the restaurant became a second kitchen, and his friends visited him there rather than at his home. He told me, "it was like our own little Cheers."[18]

Many of the respondents I interviewed stated that, although they did not necessarily enjoy being at the business, it was the only time and place they could be with their parents. They made a clear distinction between time spent with parents at the business and "quality family time," but the business was generally valued as a "second home." However, there were two young adult interviewees who consciously rejected the business and consequently distanced themselves from their parents. Susan, a Chinese American college freshman, explained: "Well, I missed my parents because they were always at the restaurant and I didn't want to go there." To reinforce her feelings, Susan worked at another Chinese restaurant owned by a competitor across the street. She stated:

I just couldn't work for my mom. I just didn't want to be with my mom. A few weeks ago, I had a talk with her and we went out to eat and everything and I said, "You know what? I don't talk to you at all. We don't talk." I go home like every two, three weeks on the weekend. I throw down my books. Go to sleep. Wake up. Go out. Come back. She's at the restaurant the whole time. I do whatever I do. She's just never around and that's it.

Susan's case is relatively extreme. Within the spectrum of acceptance and rejection, most of the respondents edged towards acceptance of their parents. On the whole, the college-age respondents provided a positive interpretation of their relationship with their parents and their childhood experience of growing up at the business. They were able to separate the difficulties they endured during their adolescence from their current perception of their parents. With hindsight, their parents are viewed as heroic figures who did the best they could under strenuous circumstances.

However, the adolescents in this study projected the lowest degree of acceptance. This is evident in the excerpts from high-schoolers Jenny and Michelle, quoted earlier. Michelle stressed how different her life was from other "American" children, how much responsibility was placed on her, and how little she received in return. In general, the adolescents expressed a common wish for boring weekends at home. They saw little value in the business. The family business was repeatedly described as a hindrance to a "normal" childhood.

Theirs is a different story than that of the older, college-age group. Maria exemplifies the different stages of development that children within immigrant entrepreneurial families experience in their relationship with their parents. She described her family business experience in this way:

Now that I think about it, it was a very positive experience. Because before the restaurant, I was very shy and I wouldn't talk to anybody. It's kind of weird 'cause when I was at the register I would be forced to talk to the customers to say "How was your meal?" Just by talking to them, I was like, "Wow, this is how you talk to people. These are people and I'm talking to them. Why can't I talk to other people like I talk to these people?" So, in a way, I feel like I've been able to adapt to more variety of people. I think that definitely increased my communication skills. Also, I think I learned about the work ethic. I know what my parents had to go through to help me along in school and everything. I learned to appreciate them a lot.

Having moved away from home for college, Maria has the luxury of hindsight in recounting her work experience. Despite having to work four, sometimes five days a week, she sees the benefits of working. However, during a follow-up interview, she described her adolescent years as "hellish," because her parents had bought another business, a small Chinese take-out, during her last year of high school. Always the optimist, she added:

> My parents have owned a restaurant since I was four. So, from seven years old on to the end of junior high, it was every Friday, Saturday night and sometimes Sundays. My parents sold it and bought another restaurant my senior year, which was pretty hellish because it was a little business just getting started so I had to go Thursday night, sometimes Friday, Saturday, sometimes Sunday, and Monday. My mom was very lenient. She let me bring my homework there. She knew I had to get it done. I had to go all the time and plus I had all those things after school.

During her high school years, intense arguments erupted between Maria and her mother, whom Maria saw as "fake" and a "hypocrite" for having one personality (i.e., polite) at the business for the customers, and another (i.e., abrasive) at home towards her.[19] Thinking back to those difficult times, Maria stated: "Well, [it's] just because of all the stress. This whole business is mentally stressful. So, it was a way to relieve all the stress. But it was all understandable. I mean we're not in conflict now. We all agreed that we need to work hard." The anger and resentment Maria felt towards her mother subsided as she began to accept the business as her own. She was able to successfully negotiate the boundaries between work and home, and childhood and adulthood. Her successful boundary work was due in part to her ability to redefine her responsibilities in a developmentally appropriate light. In Maria's case, she was able to place the same duties she had performed since she was in grade school in an adult context by viewing her role as a manager rather than as a worker at the family restaurant. She said, " . . . after a while I started training people. I figured, 'Hey, I've got some responsibility so I might as well get a word in.'" She feels a greater sense of authority in the daily management of the business. This present reinterpretation helps to soften the sharp edges of her confrontations with her parents during her adolescent years.[20]

Maria is a young adult. Adolescents, however, are usually too deeply embedded within the family and the business to search for—much less find—a story with a happy ending. For them, it is easier to simply reject the family business and disconnect from their parents. I found this to be true also for those older respondents who had no opportunity to move away from home for college. The intensely embedded nature of work and family expectations makes boundary work extremely difficult. Though these older respondents had age on their side, the other crucial elements they needed to come to terms with their alienating childhood were absent. In their scenario, the role conflicts between child and parent remain, despite the child's increasing age.

Frank, a Korean American college junior, expressed anger towards his parents. Their family business, a small construction company, had been struggling for some time. Due to their limited finances, Frank was unable to attend the college of his choice and was forced to live with his parents. When asked if he learned anything from this work experience, he replied: "I've learned annoyance and a great deal of it. And now I am basically extremely limited in terms of what I can do—school; various other things. I just don't understand how for 12 years you can continue something that's making zero money. It's ridiculous." Frank also refused to work for his parents, and after graduating, he plans to move to Korea to look for a job. In this way, he has rejected the family business and is attempting to distance himself from his parents. He consequently also rejected the core of the immigration trajectory and the "American Dream"—he seeks to reverse the process by returning to his parent's home country.[21]

Conclusion

Growing up in a small family business requires a delicate negotiation of the complex boundaries that separate work from family, and childhood from adulthood. For many of the children I interviewed, their labor is an immigrant reality and an economic necessity. Given these factors, these adolescents and young adults must create mental divisions where none exist in order to normalize or contain the differences they experience. This effort appears to be particularly difficult for adolescents who are deeply immersed in the everyday responsibilities of work and family.

Generally speaking, there have been two distinct and contradictory scholarly positions concerning the impact of small businesses on family relationships. The debate centers on whether growing up in an entrepreneurial family is a positive or negative experience for immigrant children. The first position views entrepreneurial immigrant families in a positive light.[22] Compared to immigrant salaried work, family businesses are seen as family-centered. For example, in *Longtime Californ'*, Nee and Nee present an idyllic picture of immigrant childhood that is reminiscent of *The Waltons*.[23] The authors describe a secure, family-centered childhood similar to idealistic contemporary revisionist views of pre-industrial and Depression-era families, in which everyone, including young children, works for the greater good of the household and community.[24] There is little separation between the spheres of adulthood and childhood. Nee and Nee contend that family life is integrated into the business, making the business an extension of the home. In this scenario, home life is replicated in the work environment and, provided that home life is supportive for the child, work life would also present a positive atmosphere for development.

Nee and Nee contrast the family business with salaried work. They describe working class Chinese immigrant families with salaried parents as work-centered. In this scenario, children's lives are not centered around the home. Peers become the primary socializing agent, to the detriment of family solidarity. There is apparently no sense of responsibility among these working-class children. Home life is not replicated within the work environment. In fact, they argue, there is a strict separation between home and work and between the spheres of adulthood and childhood. Their assumption here is that such an environment impedes the healthy development of children.

Light and Bonacich paint a different picture of entrepreneurial family life. In their analysis of immigrant Korean entrepreneurs in Los Angeles, they view immigrant small businesses as places of "incredible exploitation."[25] They found that 75 percent of Korean businesses employ no wage labor and require a willingness on the part of family members to work long hours for low remuneration.[26] According to the 1980 Census, more than any other ethnic group, Koreans utilized unpaid family workers.[27]

Light and Bonacich present a harsh picture of immigrant entrepreneurial life in which serious social costs are involved. For instance, they report a lack of class consciousness among small business workers due to the use of family labor. Labor disagreements often manifest themselves as family disputes rather than conflicts between workers and managers. They argue that the American dream of social mobility through entrepreneurship is a myth, and describe immigrant families as "victims of world capitalism."[28] The authors highlight the stresses these families confront and portray businesses as "dirty work."[29]

Unlike Nee and Nee, Light and Bonacich view the lack of boundaries between home/family and work as problematic. They see entrepreneurial families as work-centered, in which the parent functions as an employer or boss rather than as a father or mother. This family/work structure precludes avenues for labor disputes. In this light, some of the difficulties that may arise from a dual role of employee and daughter/son become apparent. The difficulties and stresses incurred within the business are transferred to the home, and vice versa.

These competing models of immigrant entrepreneurial life as either work-centered or family-centered do not adequately explain the intricate interrelationships within these families. I maintain that both of the above accounts of immigrant life are useful for understanding childhood in small family businesses. The boundaries between work and family are deeply enmeshed and blurred. However, neither the entrepreneurial children in this study, nor their parents, lose sight of their familial roles as daughter/sons or mothers/fathers. Rather, it is the need to play the role of family member and worker simultaneously that causes such difficulty in boundary work. The expectations of both work and family are ever-present in these children's lives, and the boundaries between the two are at times impossible to distinguish—particularly when the business is small and involves intense family labor.

The evidence provided in this study illustrates how the transition to adulthood for some children of immigrants is largely an experience of continually delayed gratification. One is not truly a child or truly an adult; rather, these developmental stages are more ambiguous in nature, as determined by the ambiguous boundaries of work and family within a small immigrant family business. The socially expected intermediate stage of adolescence is largely a luxury for such children. The developmental expectation of children and adolescents, as expressed by schools, peers, and popular culture and the media in the United States, differs from the lived experiences of these children. The family business, for these children, functions as a warped time capsule in which children grow up too fast and young adults never age.

While all adolescents may feel "abnormal" in some way, immigrant children find themselves in a unusual situation in that their "difference" is accentuated not only by their family's minority and immigrant status, but also by their involvement in small family businesses. The constraints placed upon family time and "American" versus "Asian" parenting result in particular challenges to "normality." In addition, the intense demands and embeddedness of the family business separate their childhood from that of their peers, and perhaps more important, from what these children of immigrants perceive as a "normal" American childhood. The boundary work of separating home and work, in addition to conflicting family role expectations, makes the family business and life itself especially difficult.

However, successful boundary work is important for the second generation in general: it is part of making a connection with their parents' generation while finding the individual's own place of belonging. The developmental concerns raised here highlight the importance of the *process* of growing up. Research on immigrants—and particularly the children of immigrants—has focused heavily on *outcome* measures (particularly education). However, a better understanding of the *process* of development can make a significant contribution to understanding not only the occurrence of particular outcomes or acculturation patterns, but also the formation of one's ethnic identity. The next chapter addresses some of these developmental processes in the everyday experiences of Asian Americans working at the family business.

CHAPTER FOUR

The Business in Children's Lives

I have to work all the time. I don't have time for friends, or to hang out, or just
be bored. I have to go to the restaurant after school where I cut the vegetables,
wash the dishes, and sweep the floor, then I have to take care of my younger
brothers, clean up the house and try to find time for homework. It's crazy! I
hate it! I'm so tired all the time.
—Jenny, 15, Chinese American

Asian Americans find themselves in the peculiar situation of having to
prove themselves as Americans when they already are. On the one hand
children of Asian immigrant entrepreneurs are commended as "model
minorities" for their perceived entrepreneurial "nature," while on the other
they are marginalized as foreign for the very same reason. Through examining young adults' early childhood memories of the family store, this
chapter illustrates how the family business mediates the interrelationships
within their everyday lives. These stories reveal a complex, commodified
space that disrupts normative boundaries of childhood and adulthood.

Family cohesion, in an entrepreneurial household, is understood as
essential, not only for family stability but also for their livelihood. Family
members must get along, not only to keep a family unit intact but also to
succeed in running a business in which unpaid family labor is a necessity.
For many families, the specter of downward mobility acts as a strong cohe-
sive mechanism.[1] This effect is exaggerated within entrepreneurial immigrant families, where the "family is often the main social organization sup-
porting the establishment and operation of a small business."[2] As family
members, children play an important part of this equation, and with this
role comes added responsibility. Nonetheless, little is known about how
these expectations affect adolescents and adult children who grow up in
entrepreneurial households.

In this chapter I focus on these childhood experiences. The impact of small family businesses on family life is depicted through the adult children's retelling of their early childhood memories of playing and working at the family store. Many of these children recount a common experience, problem solving and translating for their parents, starting from early childhood and continuing on to their current young adulthood. These personal accounts provide an illustrative snapshot of family life and child development that counters common expectations. This snapshot reveals a complex, commodified social environment of blurred work and family boundaries in which the usual division of "childhood" and "adulthood" is not applicable. Instead, the terms *premature adulthood* and *prolonged childhood* may best describe the lived experiences of children who grow up too fast and, as young adults, never age.

Children of Asian Immigrant Entrepreneurs

Sociological studies, reflecting the general social norm, tend to view children as priceless and incompetent.[3] This view of childhood is a relatively new social phenomenon, however. Prior to the Juvenile Justice / Child Savers movement around the turn of the twentieth century, children were often treated as little adults.[4] During the pre-industrial era, adolescence did not exist and educational demands did not postpone work and parenthood.[5] With the passage of protective legislation and the onset of industrialization, children were gradually understood to be different, both physically and mentally, from adults. In conjunction with the political and economic changes of this time, adolescence emerged as a distinctive life stage and prolonged education delayed entry into the workforce. Many children of immigrants at the turn of the century did not experience the luxury of childhood. Immigrant children were rarely spared the hardships immigrant adults endured. Their role as potential economic contributors far outweighed any sentimental adherence to notions of childhood or adolescence.

The present-day perception of children as incompetent provides little acknowledgment of immigrant children's experiences and concerns with "adult" issues such as working conditions and taxes. This neglect would lead one to assume that children and adolescents are protected from adult concerns. In entrepreneurial households, however, as much as parents try, financial security, discrimination, and familial stability are worries shared by both adults and children. Each family member experiences and expresses these worries in different ways. Song corroborates this observation in her study of Chinese young adults who grew up in small family restaurants in England. She writes, "all the young people in the sample seemed to have a heightened awareness of the precariousness of survival. Most young people were highly aware of being integral to the viability of their take-away business."[6] For these children, the business provides an intense connection to their parents and community.

In my own study, I found that despite some variation in their degree of involvement, most of the children performed regularly at the family business. Depending upon the type of business and age of the child, the respondents in my study worked as waitress/waiter, dishwasher, and checkout clerk.[7] In working at the small family business, these children experienced an altered childhood with multiple responsibilities in order to function as both "worker" (i.e., adult) and family member (i.e., child). In my interviews with Korean and Chinese American adolescents and young adults they identified some of the disjointed or inconsistent expectations placed upon them as they grew into adults. As children, they are expected by their parents to perform adult roles, and as adults, they are expected to retain the same roles they held as children. There was little change in the expectations that take into account the developmental process experienced by the young adult. More so than role reversal, role conflict, or status inconsistency, the concepts *premature adulthood* and *prolonged childhood* best describe the complexity of the lived experiences of entrepreneurial children as they make the transition from childhood to adulthood in a contested and commodified environment.

Premature adulthood is the placement of an individual who is socially considered a child (as indicated by age and developmental level)[8] in adult-like roles with adult responsibilities. Conversely, then, a prolonged childhood is the placement of an individual who is socially considered an adult in child-like roles with child-like responsibilities. The importance of both phenomena lies in the fact that they are out of synch with the larger, socially determined concept of adulthood and childhood. From the point of view of the individual in these situations, she/he is treated inappropriately in that, as a child, she/he is obligated to perform but is not rewarded for performing adult-like roles. And later, as an adult, she/he feels belittled by performing the same roles played during childhood and therefore being treated like a child by the parents. In effect, the commodification of small family businesses creates an altered environment in which children grow up too fast and, as young adults, never age.

To successfully negotiate this paradoxical situation, children from entrepreneurial families must acquire the ability to move smoothly between the status of adult/worker and child/family member at a moment's notice. Often, these children must fulfill both child and adult obligations at the same time. Though many immigrant children may experience conflicting expectations, children of entrepreneurial households have the added complexity of having to know when to switch from adult to child status within an environment in which home and work are many times inseparable.

The Small Family Business in Family Life

Kyeyoung Park argues that owning a small business is a way for immigrants to find *anjong*—establishment, stability, or security.[9] Park views anjong as the Korean immigrant model of individual success, the "Korean American Dream." She argues that business ownership is significant in transforming the lives of immigrants. For the children of these immigrants, the impact of the family business is also profound. Children who grew up in immigrant entrepreneurial households describe a family life circumscribed by the contours of the business. Daily activities revolve around the needs of the family business. Many of my respondents reported moving from one side of the city to another four or five times in their lifetime, as they switched from one form of business to another. Family vacation and family time become rare events. For many respondents, family dinners are held at 11 P.M. each evening in accordance with the closing of the store. Often, it is the only time for family members to see each other outside of the business. However, this is not to say that immigrant entrepreneurial families are simply work-centered. These children of immigrants tell a more complex, circular tale in which the needs of the business stem from the needs of the family and vice versa.

When asked if they thought their lives would be better or worse if they didn't own a family business, most of the respondents replied, "yes and no." While they each had dreamt or wished, at one time or another, that they did not have a business in their family, they were sobered by thoughts of what their life would be without it. As Jack put it, "I would probably be better off. [Pause.] I don't know. I really don't know what we would do. I don't think my dad could do anything else but run a business of his own. We'd probably be worse off." Another respondent, William, said, "It depends. If my parents were able to earn as much money by working for someone else and had more flexible and shorter hours, then yes."

During the course of the interviews, it became apparent that to say that they wished they never had a business was to disrespect their parents and the hard work and sacrifice it took to run the business. As dutiful children, they felt they must appreciate their parents and the family business for its role in providing a good future for them. It is understandable, then, that children express guilt when they admit some reservations about the business. For example, Judy said, "I think it would be better for selfish reasons. Because then I wouldn't have to work." Similarly, Robert stated: "I don't know. I think it would have been better but maybe not. There are pros and cons, I must say. I used to think that ideally my parents would be in a job that didn't require me to be there but pay just as well. That would be fine. [Laughs] That would be ideal." Another respondent simply replied, "My philosophy is that there are advantages and disadvantages; this, that, or another."

The children's matter-of-fact manner was also apparent in their discussion of what they gained and missed as a result of the business. In terms of what they gained, responsibility and maturity topped the list. Robert, a Korean American college senior, grew up in his parents' jewelry store. From a young age, he performed important "caring work" for his parents, and continues to do so.[10] He described how his labor in the family store affected his future career decision: "I think I've seen a lot of what other people do for a living, more so than maybe someone whose dad didn't include them in the business all the time. And so, I learned that there are other things that I want to try because maybe I can do it." In terms of what they missed, a "normal childhood" is at the top of almost every respondent's list. Interestingly, the same concerns that placed a burden on their lives are also presented as a benefit. For example, one of the chief reasons for their "abnormality" is heavy responsibility, which is also discussed as one of the greatest benefits of owning a family business.

Judy talked about the responsibilities and close familial connections she gained from working at the business:

> I think I've learned big lessons in responsibility. I think I feel more tied to my family. I guess I've always accepted it as part of what I see as part of my culture. Most of my friends are dry cleaner kids, and we all had the same experience. We call each other from cleaner to cleaner, "Are you out there yet? When are you getting out there?" I ended up spending a lot more time with my Korean friends than my American friends. The schedule was different. All my white American friends would hang out during the day and all the Korean kids had to work until 5:00 P.M. or 6:00 P.M. We had to go out afterwards.

Here, Judy characterizes her work experience as "culturally" Korean, given the similarities that she shares with a network of other children of Korean immigrant entrepreneurs. The business becomes a way for Judy to connect with her ethnic community. Other respondents also mentioned a greater ability to deal with a variety of people, the ability to run a business, and a greater social awareness as benefits associated with having a family store. Perhaps the most unusual benefit was one that Kyung Ah, whose family owned a jewelry store, mentioned: "I passed a class called Consumer Ed [laughs] in high school. I tested out of it because I knew how to do tax and percentages—stuff I knew because I worked at the store." Kyung Ah went on to acknowledge some of the down sides of business ownership that have had a significant impact in her life: "I think it also made me a lot more aware of things that other people didn't really think about. Like fearful things, like 'Oh, my mother can be killed tomorrow.' Things that other people didn't have to worry about that forced me to think about these things. It made me think more about how my parents will stay safe." Kyung Ah explained that she felt "set apart" from other people her age, given her fears. At one point, this fear overwhelmed her enough to seek help. She said, "I had to face these fears head-on instead of pretending that these fears didn't exist. I think that translated into the rest of my life. I think part of that has to do with how I ended up in social service." I then asked her if she felt she had missed out on certain things because of the business. She replied:

I think a carefree childhood. I think the fear of your parents being hurt is so devastating and in some ways I feel like I didn't have the power or ability to pretend that nothing was wrong. I always felt like something was wrong—even if it was in the back of my mind—I still thought about it. Sometimes it would just hit me. Or if some news would come on that some jeweler was shot to death.

Kyung Ah's sense of fear and need to protect her parents affected her childhood experiences. For her, being a child was not a carefree experience, but rather a stressful one that required attention to adult-like concerns. Robberies, while generally infrequent, are a fact of life for many small businesses. Respondents in various other types of businesses exhibit this level of concern as well. Part of their stress is derived from the shared familial understanding that if something happened to the store, it would directly affect the family. Many of the parents reportedly checked up on the family store even on their one day off a week. The business is a constant presence in the family.

Kyung Ah is not alone in her assessment of childhood. Most of the respondents lamented the loss of a normal childhood. They explicitly describe a sense of absence and sometimes even of grief. They understand the loss of a "normal" childhood as a price, as heavy as it is, for future social citizenship and opportunities. For instance, Judy said:

I think I missed out on a lot of the little things like just enjoying Saturdays and not having to feel responsible. I know my friends had the privilege of hanging out and not worrying about what their parents were doing. Or what time they had to be home. But I was always conscious of time and how much my parents would have to work because I decided to take a day off. How much more they have to work. Because they usually have to stay an hour later that night if one of us didn't go.

The direct impact of her actions on her parents is not lost on Judy. As difficult or tedious as the actual labor may be, it is the psychological and emotional connections to the parents, via the business, that make work burdensome. The children's concerns about the safety of their parents and whether or not the business will cover their daily expenses eclipse any complaints about the actual labor involved. While family vacations would be nice, most of the children simply wanted to be able to watch TV or eat a leisurely dinner with their entire family without having to jump every time a customer rang their bell. Kyung Ah summed up what she missed in this way: "Happier parents, not exhausted parents, and more family time in the evenings."

This sense of loss of a normal childhood is so deeply felt because one's childhood is intensely tied to the relationship with one's parents. There is a direct link between the child, the parent, and the family business. When the doorbell rings signaling the entrance of yet another customer, "family time" is interrupted, and sometimes altogether lost. The customer disturbs the sacred nature of "family" by reminding the child of the commercial/consumptive context of their social relationship. It is a complex environment in which the customer is both a necessity and a hindrance—and this is certainly evident in the respondents' memories of their early childhood.

Early Childhood Memories

To conclude that immigrant children's early exposure to adult-like work robs them entirely of their childhood ignores the complexities of immigrant entrepreneurial families. While not perceiving their childhood as "normal" due to the adult responsibilities, most respondents agreed that they did experience some form of childhood, albeit a different kind. In their retelling, the children were careful to present their experiences as a testament to their mothers' and/or fathers' parenting ability. The children's memories of their early years at the family business are presented as a telling example of the parents' enduring effort to provide a childhood within an adult context.

Maria's story is a poignant example. Maria recalls long days at the restaurant starting at four years of age:

> If there was a carry-out [order], my mom would start packing and make us carry it to the front so we would be walking back and forth from the restaurant. After a while, we got tired and then we got promoted, I guess. We used to do the dishes too before the dishwasher came. We had fun doing that actually. . . . For some reason there's this newspaper that did a story on our family announcing a new Chinese restaurant and there's a comment in the story that we didn't really know who our dad was because he worked so much and we never saw him, which is total *shit*. We get

along with our parents. We have our little fits here and there but nothing major. We knew we had a dad.

Maria's rendition of her childhood years is markedly different from the simplistic newspaper account. According to Maria, the business became their second home, and her father remained her father despite his long hours at the business. I asked her how she occupied her time as a preschooler. She said:

> I just played in the back. They [parents] had this office, since it was a big restaurant, and my sisters and I would draw and we'd play; and there's a park behind the restaurant so we'd go there. And actually my dad taught us how to play tennis in the back and badminton, and softball. We played paper dolls too. These Chinese soap opera characters. They made sure we were well taken care of.

Maria's family was luckier than most. Their restaurant was jointly owned with her uncle's family, providing a large pool of unpaid family labor. This arrangement offered some flexibility for "quality family time" within the business.

Others were not so lucky. However, it was apparent that these parents too made an effort to treat their young children as children, despite the tasks and responsibilities they performed. Corey and his older brother helped their mother run a Chinese take-out restaurant in a mall. He recalled his experiences growing up in a favorable light: "My family, we get along pretty well. My mom and I really get along. If I have a problem I can talk to her like a mom at the business and at home. I had to work when I was 13 years old and she would always ask me if I needed a break but she would never ask my older brother." Corey was allowed to nap after school when business was slow. He remembers falling asleep propped up against large, industrial-size soy sauce containers. Many times, he would awake with "Kikkoman" (the brand of soy sauce) imprinted on his cheek or forehead. "We all used to laugh about that," he explained, with a smile.

Most of the children began to work (i.e., they were expected to perform specific tasks) from around age 9 to age 12. Most of the children worked in the "front" dealing directly with customers. Judy had a regular work schedule by age 11: "I started working at the cleaners when I was in the sixth grade. . . . [T]hat's when they just taught me purely counter work—so I was just dealing with customers. Taking their clothes, giving them their clothes, and making change." Judy's work experience is common, particularly among the girls in my sample. They are the hostesses and counter workers, more so than their male counterparts. If there were girls or women available, the boys were expected to assist in the "back" of the store (stocking shelves, bussing tables, sweeping floors, etc.), where direct contact with customers was not necessary. The respondents were conscious of this gendered division of labor. For instance, Sally, who helped out regularly at her dad's shoe store, recounted: "I started working the register at my dad's sidewalk sales when I was about 9 years old." Her younger brother "hung out" at the store and ran errands but was not expected to deal with customers even when he reached Sally's age. Many of the girls started "working" at the family store at an earlier age than boys. These girls began as their mother's helper.

Trinh, who began to work as a pre-teen, said: "I started working for my mom at the age of 12. I was the hostess at the restaurant on the weekends." Her younger brother, who was 13 at the time of the study, had no specific job at the restaurant but was required to be there every day after school so that their parents can keep an eye on him. Kyung Ah also started working in the "front" of the store at about the same age at her parents' jewelry store. She recounted her experience:

> Now that I'm an adult, when I think about going into a store and being served by someone as young as I was, I'm kind of weirded-out by it. But no one ever felt . . . I don't remember anyone saying they didn't want me to serve them . . . but sometimes they wanted my mom to wait on them because they were familiar with her, but I've never had anyone say, "You're too young to wait on me."

Kyung Ah makes an interesting point. Not one respondent or any of their parents mentioned any concern with negative customer reactions towards child labor. In fact, the opposite generally happened. Many of the adolescents I interviewed said they had received pats on the head, figuratively or literally, from customers for being such obedient and respectful children. They usually recalled these incidents with a look of disdain—by both boys and girls. As one 16-year-old girl explained, "I hate that perfect, dutiful, Asian-girl crap. They treat me like I'm some China doll when I do a lot of hard work." As I illustrate later in this chapter, boys also expressed a sense of frustration about the lack of adequate acknowledgment of the adult-like work they perform.

This frustration is indicative of the adult-work / child-status paradox. There is uncertainty in how to reward a child for doing adult work—do you reward the child, or the work performed? On the whole, both the parents and customers tend to reward the child rather than the work. For instance, none of the children in my study were paid as if they were employees.[11] Instead, they were given "allowances" for specific (usually school-related) purchases. However, many of the children felt they were not being adequately recognized for the work they produced. Maria illustrated this point by saying:

> When I was little, I used to dream: Wow. What if [my friends] came to my restaurant and they finally knew what my life was really like. Why I can't go with them Friday night. They would realize and they'd say, "You're so cool. You have a restaurant." And they'd know about all the stuff I had to do. But that was just when I was little. Just too much day-dreaming.

Maria acknowledges the importance of peer approval to transform her business involvement into a "normal," if not a "cool," experience that others would like to do as well.

For both the parents and the children, this adult/child paradox was easier to manage during the early years of childhood, when the child performed more child-like roles, despite the adult surroundings. Robert's family illustrates this case. When I asked him what he had done at his store every day after school, he replied:

> Oh, just watch TV in the back room or whatever. There's not much for a nine-year-old to do in a jewelry store. They had the TV to keep me from being bored. Otherwise, I found other things to keep busy. [Laughs.] I used to take apart watches and that got me into a lot of trouble—when my father wasn't watching. I would take apart watches, clocks, and things that he had fixed and put on the side.

Robert's role as a child was still intact at this time. Despite his being at the store, Robert functioned as a child. This was generally the case for every respondent I interviewed. The status inconsistencies begin as the child becomes older and begins to take on more adult responsibilities on a regular basis—in other words, when the child's labor resembles work rather than a household chore. Jack described this intermediate stage, when this transformation took place:

> I was in sixth grade. That's when I started working. I started peeling shrimp at the restaurant. Doing all the grunt work and whatever dirty jobs that need to be done. Little jobs here and there. Like laundry. Me and my brother washed laundry at the restaurant. We washed dishes. Cleaning up and stuff like that. As I got older, I got more responsibilities and less of the grunt work.

Jack and his brothers never had a babysitter. The restaurant was their playground during their early years. He makes a point of differentiating those early years from working years. Simply being at the family business does not imply "working." It was not until Jack performed specific tasks in sixth grade that he described his duties as "work."

By the time children reach their teens, their chores become routinized into work. They have specific work schedules and describe their time at the business as "shifts." They also take on a title, such as waiter, hostess, or cook. In effect, they come to resemble adults/employees. This transition is difficult for both the parents and the children to negotiate. For the children, they begin to feel resentment towards their parents and their responsibilities. Judy described the frustrations she felt during this time:

> In high school, everyone had Saturdays to just hang out with their friends. Or go to the mall. I could never go. I always felt very resentful. When I was in the eighth grade through my sophomore year, I would just be so upset in the morning when my dad called . . . Well, he wants me to be at work by noon without him having to ask. And if he has to call home to ask me to come out then that's already a big deal. I've done something wrong. I would just scream and say that they are treating me like a slave. *I'm their daughter and not their worker!* [Emphasis mine.]

For most of the respondents, these feelings of resentment generally dissipate with time, maturity, and distance away from the business and family. The resentment is replaced by a sense of obligation to repay their parents' personal sacrifices. On the whole, the children, like their immigrant parents, are practical people who deal with their circumstances in a matter-of-fact manner. This attitude is apparent in the children's recounting of the work and responsibilities at the business and at home during the later stages of their childhood. The next section discusses two of the most common roles that these children performed for the family as they reached young adulthood.

Problem-Solver

For many immigrant entrepreneurs, unpaid family labor is essential to business survival.[12] These children occupied a variety of roles within the family and business, including problem-solver and translator (many times both roles at once). As mentioned earlier, only two of the families I interviewed had the luxury of shielding their children from the everyday duties of the business.

Trinh described her duties at her family's restaurant: "[I do] everything! Just kidding. I am the one who does the organizing. I supervise others when I'm there, and wait on tables, ring up checks and take orders when it gets busier." Trinh generally works for about eight hours on Saturdays, five hours on Sundays, and works on occasional Friday evenings when there is an emergency or someone calls in sick. During the summer, she works full-time. In addition to these duties, Trinh also performs latent tasks. For example, she is the family mediator, a job that is just as important to the daily operation of the business as any other. She said, "I think I'm the family's therapist, really. I set things straight for my parents and give them my honest opinions of how things can improve at the restaurant, in their lives, with family, etc. After so many years of hell with my rebellion and what not, I try to be a refreshing, peaceful entity to them [laughs], and I try to mediate and give them different perspectives."

Trinh describes a troubling adolescence filled with constant arguments with her parents, particularly her mother. She recounts those years as a time when both she and her parents "grew up" and learned from each other. Trinh explained that a few years ago her family went through a very difficult time, with her outspoken rebellion, her younger brother's repeated arrests for stealing and vandalism, and her parents' constant fighting. She said:

> They got into fights almost every night—sometimes I thought he would kill her. Another time it got so bad that my mom threatened divorce—the second time in eight years—and proposed an ultimatum for me and my

siblings to either live here or move with her to the West Coast. In the end, she decided to salvage the family, and my siblings and I got closer and decided to work as a team.

Trinh's feeling of responsibility for the business is intense, largely because she sees the business as a way of bringing and holding the family together. In this way, she feels a deep commitment to ensuring the success of the business. In addition, she feels guilty about her past role in causing stress among the family members. She presents the family business as the solution to their family problems. As the oldest of four siblings, Trinh expresses a strong sense of responsibility in modeling certain behavior and acting as a mediator in an effort to compensate for her difficult behavior during her teenage years.

The role of mediator or problem-solver is common among immigrant children. However, these roles require that, in addition to their everyday duties, children facilitate business and familial disputes. When asked what was stressful about working at the family business, most of the respondents replied that dealing with customers' negative interactions with their parents was the worst. This was evident in Judy's response to my inquiry about her involvement in the family business. She said:

> I don't really make any decisions that have to do with running the business—machines or supplies—but a few times, we've had legal problems or just daily customer problems and they asked me, "Do you think this is the American way? Am I making too big a deal with this or in your eyes, blah, blah, blah." Those kinds of decisions started coming when I was younger but now, as I'm older, they pretty much consult me with a lot of the decisions that come to the store.

When I asked how she handled these situations, she explained:

> I think I was pretty confident. I had ideas of what I thought was right and wrong. Sometimes, they would just say, "Oh, she's just a kid." But most of the time, they took me seriously. And at times that I thought it was serious enough, I told them that they needed to talk to a lawyer. So, we have this unofficial lawyer that we consult with once in a while.

In her capacity as a problem-solver, Judy functions as a cultural interpreter. She not only helps solve the problem, but also defines what is and what is not a concern. That is, she is often charged with constructing the "definition of the situation."[13] Given the seriousness of many of these issues, Judy displays a sense of confidence beyond her years. Robert, a college senior, exhibited similar attributes in his job description:

> Generally, day-to-day operations my dad can take care of now. He's got someone working with him now—Carol—who's very good being helpful to him. I tend to take care of things that arise that are problematic that Carol wouldn't know about and my dad wouldn't know about. For instance, what's going on these days is our shopping center wants to move us from where we are in the front of the shopping center because they want to put in a Cubs Food Store or something. So, they want to use that whole area. But along with that relocation, we have to make sure that all the legal documents are straight. That they are going to provide all the same things that we had in our store in the new area and that we don't have to pay for any of it. I mean that's like a two-, three-month-long thing. That's the kind of thing that I would take care of on Sundays. Things that would arise during the week that my dad or Carol couldn't take care of.

Robert confides that he feels forced to participate in the daily business operation at a level at which he feels uncomfortable. He describes his parents as "dependent" upon him and he explains that the burden this places on his shoulders is enormous.

When I asked him if he found any sense of enjoyment from working at the store, he replied:

> I think now it's more stressful than ever because I know that if I am to have a career and my own life [laughs] that I can't be this concerned with the store. Right now, I'm really concerned with this move; basically I'm making sure we're not getting screwed over by the management company. . . . I want to wean myself, and I'm trying, but every time I try to wean myself something big comes up, like this whole moving thing.

Robert vacillates from one position to another. He feels torn between his obligations to his parents and his own personal goals. His responsibilities are overwhelming, but he is at a loss to find another person willing to accept the duties. In some ways, he has a greater responsibility because he is the youngest sibling of the family. The burden is upon him to carry his parents and the family business. When I asked when he would finally feel at ease, he replied, " . . . Unless they just stopped doing the business altogether, which we have begged them to do, I'm never going to stop worrying. It's so annoying."

Later in the interview, Robert laments his decision to stay in town for college. He had hoped to move away to college and lead a "normal" student life, "where you don't have to worry so much about stuff." Unfortunately, things are never so easy. Judy, whose family owns a dry cleaning business, described her involvement with her small family business: "I end up usually doing the counter work. Interacting with the customers. I usually make phone calls if there is any kind of problem or things that have to do with English-speaking people. Even when I'm at school, they usually call me if they have problems." Judy purposely moved out-of-state for college. Like Robert, she also reports a high level of dependence on the part of her parents. The distance between her hometown and her college minimizes her parents' dependence, but not entirely. These days, Judy's parents call only when there is a problem and a mediator is required. In addition, Judy generally finds a list of chores—business- and home-related—waiting for her during her visits home (such as oil change for the car, tax questions for the accountant, vehicle registration renewal, and other bureaucratically oriented tasks).

Translator

Like many of his peers, Robert functioned in a variety of essential roles at his family's store, including acting as his parent's translator at an early age: "I was writing a lot of legal addenda to leases and stuff like that when I was 14. I remember a lawyer whom I would fax this stuff to . . . who would actually call me up and say, 'I can't believe you're only 14! If you ever want to go to law school, talk to me.'" The role of a "front person" brings with it peculiar familial circumstances. Such is the case when children become translators. Status inconsistencies may occur between parents and children in these situations. Trinh recalled her first experience as her parent's translator:

> I was my parents' translator since the age of 8 or 9 when my dad told me to talk to the plumber guy. That was a scary experience 'cause I realized that I knew something more than my dad did. It was a weird superficial sense of superiority. From then on, I translated most of their legal

papers—I remember my mom dragging me to her lawyer a couple of years ago and [telling] me to literally decipher a mass of forty documents for her within the hour. I also talk to my dad's credit card companies, deal with phone bills, gas bills, etc., etc., etc.

Trinh's "weird superficial sense of superiority" alludes to the premature adulthood she experiences. For the first time, she understood something that her father did not. She simultaneously feels proud of her newfound authority and unsure of her new responsibility as interpreter. Her senses tell her that something significant has changed in her relationship with her father, but she is uncertain about what this means.

This role-reversal may be particularly difficult for immigrant families. This situation may compound the powerlessness that many adult immigrants, particularly males, experience as a result of their new status as a racial/ethnic and linguistic minority in the United States. In light of their former position as the male head of a hierarchical household in a nation where they were the ethnic majority, Asian immigrant adult men may feel a greater loss of control.[14]

Robert, whose decision-making duties are considerable, talked about his experience of premature adulthood: "[My dad] feels like he can't make the decisions because all of a sudden after I got into college, he thinks that he's not going to be good at anything anymore. That's horrible but I can see him thinking that way." Once Robert surpassed his father's education level, he found himself in an adult role for which he was unprepared. Furthermore, he had no desire to play this part in the family business. Robert describes his relationship with his parents as "stressful." While he understands his role as a son/child, Robert never anticipated how the burden of the business would complicate his familial relationships. He was a child with adult-like worries—he was expected to deal with adult concerns at the business but behave as a child with his parents. This balance was particularly difficult to achieve during times of disagreement. Robert explained that he must present his opinions in a respectful way and comply with his parents' final decision despite what he may truly think. The boundary between adult and child is as complicated as—and is complicated by—the boundary between work and family.

This was also the case for Kyung Ah. She recalled several instances when she intervened as translator:

The only times I can think of is when there is a misunderstanding between a customer and my parents. Something about just the way my mom was saying something would come off the wrong way and I would step in if I was there and just kind of explain. . . . I think my mom's English just got worse if she got excited and angry. So I would just step in and be calm and try to settle the situation.

Like her peers, Kyung Ah must mediate in times of stress. She functions as a cultural bridge between her parents and the customer. To do this, she must show deference to her parents while exercising her authority as an English speaker. Jack recalled similar circumstances: "I handled advertisements, I dealt with lawyers, customers, stuff like that. I think that, as kids of our parents, that was one of our main jobs. I think all of us [did that], not just those of us in the restaurant business. All immigrants." Jack is matter-of-fact about his translator role. In fact, he views this role as a *child's* responsibility.

Today, growing numbers of adolescents are working in the service economy, where there is a proliferation of part-time jobs requiring little skill and that allow them to work at "off" hours.[15] Most of the teenagers in this economy are white, middle-class, and residents of suburbs; their primary motivation for working is no longer their family's financial need, but to have income for discretionary purchases.[16] This experience is different from that of immigrant children, who are many times unpaid and work in a family business where child labor laws do not apply. More important, their labor is not discretionary but required for family survival.

Betty Lee Sung, in her early study of Chinese immigrant children, writes, "[A] reversal in parent-child roles is a frequent occurrence in Chinese American homes, especially those where the parents are not well educated and do not speak English."[17] However, this reversal may be exaggerated within an entrepreneurial setting in which the parent is dependent upon the child to provide translation or mediation, often on a daily basis. The role of the translator requires more than language proficiency. To act as a cultural bridge, one must also be an astute observer, particularly in times of stress. Scholars of color have discussed the ability of (and necessity for) minorities to juggle several spheres of knowledge in order to successfully navigate among different, and sometimes contradictory, worlds.[18] This is also true for immigrant children. At an early age, immigrant children become savvy cultural negotiators. However, there may be costs incurred by achieving this ability. There is the danger that the pressures of an adult role may hinder a child's development.[19] There is also concern for the parents' ability to demonstrate authority and adult modeling. A *New York Times* article illustrates this issue: "As more children take on the role of interpreter for those who do not speak English . . . social workers here say that because children play an adult role in doing the translating, they may grow up too quickly and resent or lose respect for their parents."[20] The disruption caused by premature adulthood may be a demeaning and uncomfortable phenomenon for both parties, who must now manage a different relationship.

Searching for a Carefree Childhood

During the interviews, the children were careful to present a balanced picture. For every missed opportunity, they mentioned something they gained from growing up in a small family business. Their years of experience as a cultural interpreter have helped foster maturity and practicality. As the bridge or mediator between two different cultures, these children have carefully juggled a variety of responsibilities. They have also negotiated several different roles—including problem-solver and translator—that have forced them to shift from child to adult roles depending on the social context.

This shifting of roles and responsibilities requires a great deal of energy and thought. Perhaps what makes childhood "carefree" is the absence of such expectations. The children in this study were astute in finding bits and pieces of childhood in different social contexts. For instance, they found childhood in "outside" work (e.g., a job unconnected to the family business—McDonald's, etc.) and school. Both outside work and school are viewed as a reprieve from the adult world with its adult worries.

Both of these institutions, as paths to greater mobility, are allowable reasons for not working at the family store. However, there are significant differences between the two. Not all parents allowed their children to have outside jobs. Those who were open to this found only particular jobs acceptable, and then only during the summer, so that neither their education nor their time at the family business would be affected. Robert worked for a federal government agency during the summer: "My parents were very happy about that. I was really surprised that they let me do it. I didn't think they would know what I was talking about. I mean it's strange how my parents know about particular things. I thought they weren't aware of anything else but the top ten list of colleges."

Jobs that parents viewed as educational or that exposed their children to the "real" world were deemed acceptable. Generally, it appears that acceptable real-world representations are those that supported the parents' view of life. For instance, Tony, a Korean American college junior, discussed his parents' reaction to his summer jobs. "I had summer jobs before and my parents were all for it because my parents thought that I should learn about the full work day in the 'real' world." Tony's parents wanted their son to better understand some of the conditions under which they worked.

Beth, an 18-year-old Chinese American, replied that her parents felt the same way. "They wanted me to experience the outside world. Like in the real world, not just working for your parents." There is an "unreal" quality to working for one's parents, given the unclear boundaries between work and home, employee and daughter, and adult status and child status. In addition, the parents do not view the children's activities at the business as work. To them, the children are simply helping out, just as they would if they were at home.

School—whether it is high school or college—also has a "carefree" association for immigrant entrepreneurial children. It is a place where they are expected to be immature adolescents. It is also a place with friends their age. Many of these children looked forward to Mondays, after a difficult weekend of hard work. One student recalled his high school days. "I used to make up school things to do. In high school, it was debate practice so that I didn't have to go to the store on some afternoons after school." This is common among entrepreneurial kids. Many are involved in five or six different extracurricular activities. They understand that only education-related reasons would excuse them from work. Jack described his experience growing up: "I didn't have to work on test days. Actually, the day before a test. That's generally the only day I get off. Or if I'm feeling really sick one day. Well, if it's not a busy day, I'll take the day off. But on weekends, I'll work even if I'm sick. It's too busy."

Other students recounted similar experiences. Bob replied: "I think school was a big thing. My parents tried to live vicariously through us so if the word 'school' came up, that was it. It was amazing. Anything that was needed for school was right there. They would bend [over] backwards for whatever school purposes there were." However, given their work schedules, the parents were rarely involved in routine school functions. Most of them did not attend school events; nor did their children ask them to. As one student put it, "They know what it looks like generally but that's 'cause they had to meet me there a couple of times." As much as education was stressed, it was solely the child's responsibility. Judy explained: "They pretty much trusted me to deal with school on my own. If I needed anything, they would be a resource in terms of financially. Like if I wanted to take a prep course or some kind of enrichment thing, but basically I had to figure out everything for myself." Given the intense involvement of parents in other facets of their lives, they see school as an escape to a child-like, carefree environment. While they may occasionally wish their parents could attend an orchestra concert or other school activities, they generally expressed relief to have some space of their own.

In the next chapter I will analyze how these children of Asian immigrant entrepreneurs manage to create some space to call their own through narratives of their family's immigration history that are eerily reminiscent of the classic American Western. This narrative becomes an important ideological mechanism to deal with the exoticized stereotypes that surround their family's business.

CHAPTER FIVE

The American Narrative of Asian Immigration

> My family immigrated for better opportunities. They don't talk much about
> [it]. During the first few years, my dad was homeless for a while in New York,
> living in Times Square for a while. He couldn't find a job, so he lived on the
> streets. I don't think it was too long. He usually uses it to teach us lessons. He
> doesn't really show any emotion when he talks about it. . . . That's about all
> they will say about it.
> —Sam, a 19-year-old Korean American

> Go West, young man . . . strike off into the broad, free West, and make yourself
> a farm from Uncle Sam's generous domain.
> —Horace Greeley, editor of the *New York Tribune* (1867)

The immigrant narrative, as articulated by children of immigrants, represents a particular understanding of the reasons for leaving one's homeland and the experiences upon arrival in another. There are two striking initial patterns in the children's retelling of their family's migration to the United States. First, the children know very little about the actual experience of their parents' decision to emigrate and their experiences upon arrival. Second, regardless of how little knowledge the children do possess, their stories are remarkably similar to each other regardless of their ethnic and class background. This chapter focuses on the children's retelling of these stories as an important indicator of the particular political and economic context in which these children of immigrants find themselves. First, I argue that the second generation utilizes three variations of the classic Western narrative in describing their parents. Second, I establish the American origins of the immigrant narrative. And, third, I discuss the significance of gendered narratives associated with Asian immigrant labor in determining how Asian Americans view their social position.

These immigrant narratives, which function to normalize their presence, are fundamental to understanding why second generation Asian Americans feel compelled to remind others of their existence in the United States and how they go about doing so. Consequently, it is no coincidence that these stories follow a distinctly "American" narrative construction: in it, their entrepreneurial parents play the part of classic Western heroes, regardless of the actual financial outcome of the small family business. These heroes are brave individuals, who courageously overcome seemingly insurmountable odds to become *productive* American citizens. Whether or not the family business consistently turns a profit each year, it requires intense work and labor input, particularly in the early years of migration, exemplifying the pioneering character of these men and women. The narrative constructs "the good immigrant" as deserving of social citizenship rights based upon their productive worth to the larger society. It sees the social context of immigrants as a commodified environment in which their acceptability is measured by their willingness to devote their lives to the economic engine of their new nation without complaint. The reward for such sacrifice is "opportunity" for their children to experience upward economic mobility, as evidenced by their conspicuous consumption.

The Asian Immigrant Entrepreneur as Classic Western Hero

As a film genre, early Western narratives starting in the late 1800s (*Cripple Creek Barroom*) and continuing through the 1950s (*My Darling Clementine*) present a powerful vision of America as an uncivilized frontier that is conquered by a lone individual. Carl Bredahl notes that the traditional representation of the West, as best exemplified by John Ford's films (*My Darling Clementine, Stagecoach, Fort Apache, She Wore a Yellow Ribbon,* etc.), is a racialized vision. The West is presented as vulnerable to incivility and in need of protection by "the white man" and his values; as opposed to Indians, who are portrayed as threatening the land.[1] Frequently, this heroic individual is a courageous male figure who does not speak much, is rarely emotional, and overcomes seemingly insurmountable odds in the pursuit of goodness. Variations of this narrative followed, including the semi-classic version of the 1950s (e.g., *High Noon*), which was less positive and more ambivalent towards civilization.[2] But, regardless, the cowboy remains an American hero. Richard A. Maynard writes, "Daring, noble, ethical, romantic, he permeates our popular media to this very day. He personified our national self-image—the conqueror of wilderness, savagery, and villainy. He is America's knight-errant with a Colt 45." He goes on to point out, "Our fascination with this mythical figure and the great plains he is alleged to have conquered has nothing whatsoever to do with the actual history of the American West."[3] It is an optimistic, fictional story in which the good guy always wins in the end. It is also a quintessentially American construction that serves as a powerful normalizing tool for the children of immigrants as they present themselves as legitimate citizens worthy of all the social rights bestowed upon "Americans." Its storyline is a familiar one in the immigration narratives of the second generation.

These immigration stories have three basic characteristics in common with the classic Western narrative. First, the parent (usually the father) is the hero, a lone individual who could not work for anyone else. Regardless of the actual mobility outcomes of the family and business, the parent is characterized as the hero who endures mental and physical hardships to persevere. This facet of the story sustains the traditional gendered hierarchical structure that defines individual familial roles. Regardless of the responsibilities placed upon the child, the parent, particularly the father, maintains the breadwinner role, and filial piety is kept intact within this narrative. In addition, this Western narrative functions to "Americanize" the parents, by not only masculinizing the father but also "westernizing" the mother. This requires making the mother a contemporary American superwoman who is empowered by successfully juggling both work and family.

Second, the story has a happy or satisfying ending. Again, each narrative fashions an optimistic ending regardless of seemingly objective measures of (business) failure. Given the porous division between family and work, to admit business failure is to imply family failure. Also, a happy ending is an important component in developing an explanation for all the difficulties and hardships endured during and after migration. In this way, the ending justifies the parents' decisions, including the decision to immigrate to the United States. In addition, the ending has deep significance for the children, who hear repeatedly, throughout their life, that everything—both good and bad—was done for them. In this regard, they are the final chapter of this immigration story.

Third, the stories employ the familiar theme of the struggle for survival. There are three variations on this theme: (1) rags to riches, (2) martyrdom, and (3) morality. Respondents choose a particular variation, based upon how, in their eyes, their current material success (there is no failure in these stories) measures up to what they envision their parents had upon emigration or prior to owning the family business.[4]

Rags to Riches

The first theme is the most familiar immigrant and entrepreneurial story. Rags to riches is the American dream of self-made success. There are a number of individuals whose life story is frequently presented in accordance with this popular American lore. Andrew Carnegie is one of the most familiar figures for this purpose. Carnegie emigrated from Scotland with his family in 1848. At the age of 14, he obtained his first job as a messenger boy in a Pittsburgh telegraph office. He rose from this "lowly" position to steel magnate before the century was over. He was often quoted as endorsing the "advantages" of being "reared in the stimulating school of poverty."[5] Poverty, then, is romanticized as a temporary, character-building experience for those strong-willed enough to pull themselves out of it.

Similarly, Supreme Court Justice Clarence Thomas was presented to the media as "a man whose very life exemplifies the American dream" by then Senate Minority Leader Bob Dole. Thomas, the grandson of a black sharecropper who rose from poverty in segregated Georgia, has stressed his personal initiative in rising above poverty, comparing himself with his sister, Emma Mae Martin, a single mom raising four children on welfare. He said, "[My sister and her kids] have no motivation for doing better or getting out of that situation." Later accounts noted however that while her brother was attending Yale Law School, Martin, who had been abandoned by her husband, worked two minimum-wage jobs to support her children. Later, an elder aunt who provided childcare for the kids suffered a stroke. Martin received welfare for four and a half years to care for her children and her aunt. Another who is also said to embody the American Dream is Oprah

TABLE 5.1
Typical Immigrant Entrepreneurial Narratives

Theme	Distinguishing Characteristics	Mobility Trajectory
Rags to riches	Meager origins, abundant outcomes	Upward
Martyrdom	Abundant origins, meager outcomes	Downward
Morality	Modest origins, modest outcomes	Flat

Winfrey, the richest woman in the entertainment industry. The fact that she is a Black woman born in poverty on a small farm in Mississippi makes her story of success that much more powerful. There are, of course, other celebrities whose story seems to fit this archetypal mold. Each began with little except their "bootstraps." The story goes that they created incredible success from sheer hard work and determination. Their mobility trajectory is off the chart. Understandably, it makes an attractive model for immigration stories. It places foreign or marginal characters within the center of a quintessentially American story. In this way, it enables the children of immigrants also to stake their claim as Asian *Americans*.

Robert recalled his own family's immigration story using this motif of rags to riches:

> My father immigrated to the United States first. He came to Chicago because other friends of his were also coming here at the time. After the [Korean] war, my dad was poor and couldn't afford an education. Without an education, he knew that there was no room for upward mobility in Korea so he left. Once he got here, he got a job as an apprentice with a friend who was a jewelry maker. Then he sent for the rest of us. He worked there until he saved enough to buy his own store. My dad's really thankful for what he's got. He's not like other Korean business owners he knows who resent their station in life. He doesn't see himself as downwardly mobile. He knows that he couldn't have done any better in Korea.

Robert's parents had little formal education when they came to this country. They now have two businesses (one of which has not turned a profit in five years), three well-educated grown children (two of whom have professional degrees), and live in a comfortable suburban home. A similar story was told by Trinh, whose parents are Chinese. The entire family emigrated from Vietnam in 1981. In Vietnam, Trinh's father's family owned an herb shop while her mother's family sold vegetables and fruits from a small market stand. When I asked Trinh why they chose to open a Vietnamese and Chinese restaurant, she replied: "It's always been my mother's dream to have something of her own. My mom was the 'brain' of the whole operation actually. She's so entrepreneurial that she bought two apartments and co-signed them with other relatives."

Having something of one's own or being a boss (despite that fact that they are the boss of only their family members) is an important theme and works to strengthen the hero image. While many of my respondents realize that their parents became small business owners more out of necessity rather than choice, they appear to find comfort in the idea that their parents were somehow different from those who follow other people's orders. During a follow-up interview, I asked Trinh if she thought her life would be better or worse if her family did not own a business. After some thought, she said: "I think that my parent's business was a realization of a dream since they fled from Vietnam. And I am so proud of them for being able to do what others could only dream about." In this case, Trinh's mother occupies the hero role more than her father. It is fitting, since her mother came from a significantly poorer background. Despite the fact that her mother's most recent restaurant venture failed, the mother embodies the American dream. Certainly, the family has experienced significant upward mobility from their humble origins in Vietnam.

Having arrived in the United States at the age of 4, Trinh too identifies strongly with her own immigrant background. Her use of the rags-to-riches narrative to describe her own accomplishments illustrates this. At 19 years of age, Trinh describes herself as "financially independent" of her parents:

> This year I paid off almost all of my tuition through the numerous scholarships I worked for during my senior year in high school. I took care of all the financial details of college. What was left was tuition and room and board of less than $1,600—which I asked that they [parents] pay for. Every time I came back to ask for a portion of that money, I got hell from

them 'cause they thought I should also pay for that amount myself. I tell them, though, that I am already paying my living expenses through my work-study [job] and through some of the tip money I make on the weekends working for them. I could have worked at another restaurant on the weekends but I decided that was the best way to earn money and see my family too. I also charged any recreational stuff or gifts or purchases on my credit cards, which I pay promptly every month. I guess my main point is that they don't realize how difficult it's been for me to reduce the tuition and at the same time live on money made from work-study and the restaurant.

Certainly, what Trinh has done is no small feat. She attends an expensive private university and is obviously proud of her success. Her description of the hardships and sacrifices she endured is also an element found in the second variation of the survival theme, martyrdom.

Martyrdom

The primary difference between the rags-to-riches and martyrdom narratives is a negative mobility slope. Unlike the rags-to-riches narrative, the martyrdom narrative begins with abundant origins and ends with meager outcomes. However, martyrs are not considered failures; rather, they are heroes, in that they endure great sacrifices and suffering for the sake of a principle or cause. The parents in this category had generally enjoyed a higher social status in their native country. Such is the case for Jane, whose father was once a mechanical engineer in Korea, and in the United States bought a shoe store in a low-income, inner-city neighborhood. Since 1978, her family has attempted to run four different stores—a beauty supply store, a shoe store, a video store, and finally their current shoe store. The family has endured one business failure after another. Jane matter-of-factly told me, "I feel that my parents had to sacrifice more and work harder because they had a business." She continues to feel a sense of obligation to her parents to repay their sacrifices and describes her relationship with them as "close."

Alice's parents, too, enjoyed high social status prior to immigration. Her father was a physician and her mother graduated with an art degree from a prestigious Korean university. They now own a dry-cleaning business in a working-class suburb. Alice explained: " . . . they used to have regrets about not doing what they really wanted to do in life and they have very little time to do what interests them. All their free time goes to church, where my parents are very active—my mom's a deaconess or something, and my dad is an elder—and resting." When asked how she felt about working at the family dry cleaners, she replied, "It's good for me to learn how to work hard. It gives me a good work ethic since it's such hard work and it makes me learn to appreciate my parents working for me." Within this narrative, the hero sheds his/her material things for his/her spiritual convictions. In fact, Alice even stated that her parents work *for her.*

Peter, a Korean American college student, worked at his parent's import-export business one summer. He told me: "It was a good experience. I got to see my parents in a different light. You get used to them in a certain light and it's good to see them as others do. You get an appreciation for what they do to put you in school. It makes school even more important." Maria expressed similar sentiments about her parents. "I know what my parents had to go through to help me along in school and everything. I learned to appreciate them a lot." She went on to add:

> I think [my father] opened it [the restaurant] just because he knew we were going to college and he needed some sort of income to provide the money for it. He always wanted us to go to college and he also supported my uncle, his younger brother, through college. My dad knew how important college is. He has a high regard for education. That's why when my uncle graduated, he gave my dad his class ring.

Their parents stress the importance of education in a variety of ways. Strong evidence for this is that the children reported that school-related activities were one of the only reasons (along with illness) their parents allowed for not working at the business.

The sense of parental sacrifice for the benefit of the children's education was also apparent when the respondents discussed whether or not they found working at the family business stressful. Seventy-six percent (fifty-four out of seventy-one) of the respondents stated that they found working at the family business stressful. The most common source of their stress was interactions between the customers and their parents. In general, the children related that they witnessed few outright racist or otherwise derogatory comments or behavior by customers towards their parents. Instead, they frequently observed a more subtle tone of condescension.[6] Angela, whose family owns a coin laundromat, responded, "There are some crazy customers who come in. They just slam the door really hard and sometimes they break them. We have to deal with angry customers. It's really hard." She added that what she found most stressful about these encounters was watching how the disgruntled customers spoke to her parents. She said, "They're so disrespectful. I can tell that they think my parents are stupid immigrants." Another respondent, Linda, spoke about some of the more stressful interactions she witnessed: "My mom is really good with people. She's really . . . sometimes overly nice but sometimes customers get really pissed and start yelling about some stupid thing. It's really painful." Other times, they noticed condescension by customers during "positive" interactions. Young, an 18-year-old Korean American, explained: "I find dealing with customers stressful. I can tell when they're treating my parents like they're kids. They talk really slow. I almost feel like they're going to pat them on the head for a job well done. It makes me sick." He went on to remind me that his father has an advanced degree in mechanical engineering and his mother was a college professor prior to migration.

In these stories, the parents are portrayed as martyrs for their self-sacrifice for the sake of others. Their sacrifice is most often understood as the loss of social status and the consumptive goods that signify social location. Small family business ownership is understood as a lowly profession and one of downward mobility. The parents are portrayed as having to function below their actual level of intellectual and social ability. To compensate for this negative trajectory, the meaning of work and labor within the business is elevated beyond the tangible everyday world. The work and labor of mothers and fathers signify a greater meaning—that of the all-giving (heroic) parent whose life is devoted to a "greater" good—the child's future.

Morality

The third narrative type is the morality tale, which is similar to a fable in that it is cautionary. In it, the pattern of mobility is held constant. Modest origins prior to migration result in modest outcomes. There is little change in mobility. The moral to this story is "work hard and do not be greedy." There is no significant success or failure, but the heroes are good, honest people. Ben told such a story when I asked why his family decided to move to Philadelphia:

> It's where my uncle's family lived. Later, my uncle's family moved to [a wealthy suburb]. At the time, it seemed like the way to success because my uncle's family lived in Philly, started a business, and then he made more money, started another business, and then moved to the suburb. It seemed like that's the way it worked. But that was the seventies. It's kind of different now; the neighborhood is different too. By the time we moved in [to Philly], it was a bit poorer, not as safe, and the economy was different. We didn't follow the same progression that my uncle did.

I then asked how quickly his uncle moved out of the city. He replied: "Pretty soon considering that my family is still in the city—twelve years now. They were probably in the city for only half that time. The thing is that now he's sort of struggling now to make ends meet. The recession hit him hard. Sort of like the 80s boom and then . . ." While his uncle sped hastily towards upward mobility—à la rags to riches—Ben's father remained in the city, working hard in his small dry cleaners for twelve years.

Christine, whose family has managed a swap meet for the last five years after "trying out" four other businesses, tells a similar story: "It's been standing for longer than any of the other businesses that my parents have had. It is a steady income." Don, whose parents own a video store, said, "It's the longest-running business in Koreatown. It has its ups and downs. My parents work really hard at it." Christine and Don both describe their parents as "satisfied" with their life but not necessarily happy. And, like others who incorporate the morality theme in retelling their stories, Christine and Don categorize both themselves as steadily "middle-class" and characterize their parents as generally content with their station in life.

The three narratives are not mutually exclusive, but each has its own set of distinctive characteristics. In retelling their stories, the interviewees were thoughtful and astute in their comments. Without seeming naive, each person appeared to take comfort in their narrative's normative effects. For these Asian Americans, these narratives, with their variant themes, function to create a sense of connection with and understanding of their Asian parents. In addition, these narratives function to reinforce their own presence as legitimate Americans.

The Immigrant Narrative as an American Construction

In the end, the immigration stories told by the children of immigrants are more about themselves than about their parents. They are important re-creations of who they are and why they do what they do. However, the parents are a crucial link, providing the significant details—as few and far between as these clues may be—to make these narratives "real." Since the majority of the children were very young during migration or were born in the United States, they rely primarily upon their parents for any information regarding this important period in their lives; however, details are relatively rare and intermittently provided. For instance, Joe, a 19-year-old from Chicago, told me: "We don't talk about our migration experience. We all understand that we rather prefer here than Korea." There is a sense of filial piety[7] implied in Joe's statement. To talk about migration has the potential to bring up painful events and perhaps even question the parents' decision to emigrate. For Dean, another Korean American college student, *not* talking about this experience is understood as culturally "Korean." He said, "My mom keeps telling me that she did it, like most Asian families, because their family always comes first. I think they did it for just the children, to get a better education and opportunities. . . . They don't talk about it too much. I kind of expect them to, but they don't. American families, the parents will talk about the hard times, but not Koreans." To talk about difficult—and perhaps even traumatic—matters would disrupt what appears to be an implicit "don't ask, don't tell" policy in family interaction.

Only 11 percent (n = 10) of the total sample of eighty-eight respondents (both entrepreneurial and non-entrepreneurial) said that they knew "a lot" about their family's migration experience. Upon further probing, it was evident that most of this small sub-sample did not actually know a great deal about the details but rather had heard the same few generalities (i.e., the difficulty of immigration) repeated throughout their lives. Every respondent interviewed described his or her family's migration experience as "hard" or "difficult."

These children have come to rely on indirect sources to accumulate bits and pieces of their family's history. Christine told me: "My family immigrated because there were more business opportunities and the rules in America aren't as strict as they are in Korea. But I'm not quite sure." When asked about her parents' early years after immigration, she said, "They weren't middle-class then. When I see pictures I don't see a lot of nice furniture in the apartment they lived in. They don't really talk about it." Here, Christine constructs a narrative using photographs as family artifacts. Other times, children construct their history by overhearing adult conversation. When asked, Chow said, "They don't talk about their migration experience very much. My parents talk to my grandparents and my uncles and aunts about it, but they don't really talk to the children about it." The parents appear to want to protect their children from the difficult periods of their lives. What details they do divulge is purposeful, in that they share particular information to fulfill their child's school assignment or provide a life-lesson of some sort. Otherwise, the children are largely left to their own devices in constructing a narrative of why they are here and, more important, why they *belong* here.

One respondent, Jin, knew more than most about his parent's early experience in the United States:

> They immigrated for economic opportunity and partly a sense of adventure. The first few years were very difficult. They came with about $2,000 in their pockets. . . . My dad's friend's brother was living in San Francisco, so they went there. They were greeted by a Korean friend of a friend who invited them to their apartment to adjust. There were a lot of other Korean men living in small apartments until they got jobs and were settled. My mom was pregnant with my brother. As the only woman in this all-men household, she had to cook and clean for everyone. It wasn't what she expected from America. My dad had said he would take care of her and they would have a great marriage and she wouldn't have to work. And here she was waking up at 4 A.M. to cook for these gentlemen. This was their honeymoon. She would cry a lot at night. She had her baby and all the men were always using the bathroom.

One of the reasons why Jin knew more than most is that he was required to interview his parents as part of a school project. This was also the case for Tim, who sat down with his parents for the first time for an assignment for an ethnic studies course in college. He said: "You can see your parents' experiences through the books, like chronologically where they fit in. . . . I really never talked to my parents about it before. Reading and taking classes definitely got me thinking. I wouldn't even have wondered. I was born here. I just figured that they just got to come here." After this experience, Tim switched his major from economics to ethnic studies.

These immigrant narrative constructions have a generic or formulaic quality to them, in that the stories could describe almost any immigrant group in almost any historical period. It is the familiar, quintessentially "American" story about poor immigrants who come to the United States— the land of opportunity—and through sheer determination and hard work make something of themselves (i.e., melt into the pot). This is, in fact, an important ideological construction of the creation of the United States as the "land of immigrants"; in it, the United States plays the role of the savior who rescues the tired, the poor, and the oppressed of the world. This narrative perpetuates the invisibility of conquest, slavery, and the exploitation of both labor and natural resources that were institutionally imposed throughout the process of nation building.[8] For the children of immigrants, it is a vision of a mythical and patriotic America that works to prove, once again, that Asian Americans are indeed part of a whole—as Americans.

However, these immigrant narratives have a double edge.[9] To make this image work, Asian Americans must perpetually perform the foreigner role in order to be "discovered," "welcomed," and "domesticated" again and again. Doing so is required of all "good" minorities.[10] This narrative is tautological in design. Asian Americans, as "marginal others" trying to establish their legitimate presence as citizens, are compelled to insert their familial history into an orientalist drama that requires that they play the foreigner, over and over again.

And yet, the story continues. The immigrant narrative is a powerful draw, not only for Asian Americans but also for anyone who wants to believe in the American Dream. The ubiquitous nature of this story is inescapable. For the Asian American second generation, the appeal of this narrative is its ability to reaffirm one's social citizenship through a quintessentially American lens, thereby "normalizing" differences that mark Asian Americans as outsiders or foreign. The young adults in their discussion of the work and labor of their parents particularly emphasized this process of normalization.

The next section of the chapter will analyze the initial sense of gendered stigma that the children experienced and how they have incorporated a specific immigrant entrepreneurial narrative to "normalize" this stigma. I will argue that this social stigma is a result of the historical feminization of domestic service sector labor. I will also discuss the racialized construction of Asian American masculinity and femininity.

Gendered Narratives of Asian Immigrant Labor

Ben, a Korean American college freshman, grew up in a large metropolitan city in a working-class, African American neighborhood. He lives with his father, mother, and younger brother in an apartment above the dry cleaners that his father runs. His mother works at a garment factory in a nearby neighborhood. In describing how he felt about the family business, Ben recalled an incident that stayed with him for years:

> Well, in elementary school I didn't really think about [the store] much. When I got into junior high school and high school-—it was one of those special schools where you had to take a test to get in—there were people from all over the city and most of these people were better off than me. I came in contact with middle- and upper-class students basically for the first time. I became conscious of the lower status of dry cleaners and garment factory workers. I remember one experience in Spanish class, we were doing exercises—talking—and everyone had to talk about what their parents did—so you get these impressive jobs like a journalist for the newspaper or somewhere. I felt good at the time that I didn't have to speak. They didn't call on me. It felt kind of weird to say that my parents were, you know, had typical immigrant jobs.

The "weird" feeling that Ben describes is the sense of stigma that is associated with service sector and light manufacturing jobs—or "typical immigrant jobs." I argue that what makes these "typical immigrant jobs" so demeaning is not only that they are considered unskilled or manual labor but also that they are traditionally associated with women's work. Immigrant work has historically been gendered as "female," and therefore degraded as undesirable or inappropriate for "real" men.

The incident in Spanish class occurred when Ben was in the seventh grade. It was not until his senior year in high school that Ben began to feel more comfortable with his family's source of livelihood. Ben credits this transformation to a history lesson: "I learned, later in high school, about earlier immigrant groups. I learned about what Italians and Jews experienced earlier in this century. It sounds very similar to what my father was doing. I didn't think anymore that it was some kind of lowly job." Ben placed his parents in the larger social context of American history. He transformed his family's business from a nondescript sweatshop in a poor neighborhood to a site of dignity and a tradition of hard work—a place from which he could derive a sense of pride.

When I asked interviewees what their parents did for a living, they usually initially exhibited a heavy sense of reservation and precaution. Some were immediately defensive and asked, "Why do you ask?" in response. When I explained my purpose and the fact that I too grew up in a small immigrant family business, their body language changed and they were more open to questions. Others gave me an almost embarrassed smile, and replied, "Oh, you know, they own a small business, the usual immigrant job." It was obvious that these responses were pat answers composed in advance. Rather than make the energy-intensive effort to confront racist, classist, or sexist notions of Asian immigrants, these students avoided the issue through lighthearted acknowledgment and dismissal of existing stereotypes.

However, it is not always so easy. Watching one's parents in subservient positions is difficult. One college freshman, Carrie, spoke of a painful moment in her relationship with her parents: "I used to be very embarrassed of them for speaking with an accent, or when they acted *too* humble for their own good, too nice and quiet around white Americans, etc., or so scared whenever a dark-skinned person approaches. For the past few years I've walked in their shoes and feel ashamed for being embarrassed by them before." I asked what she meant by "walking in their shoes." She replied:

Walking in my parents' shoes means being more empathetic; or developing more empathy over the years as I have grown up from a more "I'm suffering, I'm alone . . . so alone in this world . . . pitiful me . . . pitiful me" to a young woman who sees others' pain and accepts life with its strong and weak points and tries to look inside my parents' head and heart and try to understand why they think or do things a certain way. I think, in our constant arguments, my parents began to "walk in my shoes" as well to see why I do certain things.

The fact that Carrie's parents seemed to embody some of the stereotypes that are associated with Asian immigrant entrepreneurs made her very uncomfortable, and she found herself viewing her parents as a foreigner. Part of Carrie's development was to separate the racial stereotypes associated with their occupation from her parents. Her sense of discomfort dissipated as she began to understand her parents' behavior as normal rather than strange or different. Particular American narratives, as a normalizing agent, perform an important function in doing this.

The Gendered History of Asian Immigrant Labor

Immigrant small family businesses are part of the growing service sector in today's economy.[11] Since the onset of deindustrialization, this economic sector has grown to include more male workers displaced from traditionally blue-collar male labor markets such as manufacturing. This sector has also expanded its range of jobs by including high-paid white-collar consultants. However, the service economy continues to uphold its traditional persona as a female market place. Low wages, low status, and general lack of worker autonomy are hallmarks of traditional female occupations.[12] As part of this market sector, immigrant small family businesses share these "feminine" characteristics. These families are merchants who serve other people. Asian immigrants have held this subservient position in America for quite some time.[13] For instance, the first Chinese laundry was established in the mid-1800s on the Pacific Coast.[14] Chinese men entered the traditionally *female* domestic labor market as the gold mines dried up and manual labor was no longer needed on the railroads. This move into domestic work came out of necessity rather than choice.

As sojourners, Asian men migrated to the United States as laborers. Chinese men were the first to enter in substantial numbers. They intended to earn money in the United States and return to their families in their home country. Consequently, Chinese women remained in China. Later, immigration laws prohibited their entrance to the United States.[15] There were fears that if the women were admitted, the Chinese would shift from sojourners to permanent residents once their labor was no longer needed.

Initially, the Chinese immigrants had intended to enter traditional male occupations such as mining, construction, and later farming in the new frontier. There were two specific economic and social factors that contributed to their movement into domestic work. First, several significant economic changes occurred during the late 1800s. Jobs became scarce in the West as mines closed and railroads were completed. In 1861, over 50 percent of all Chinese immigrants were employed by mining companies. In addition, of the twenty-five thousand mechanics and laborers hired by the Central Pacific Railroad Company, fifteen thousand were Chinese.[16] The closing of both of these industries had a devastating effect on Chinese migrants. Second, several social factors also pushed Chinese men into female markets. There were few women—white or otherwise—in the new frontier. Communities of male miners and laborers either did their own domestic chores or, more likely, neglected them altogether. Within these communities, there was a great demand for household and personal services such as washing clothes and cooking.[17] Also, there was an onslaught of anti-immigrant—and specifically anti-Chinese—sentiment at the end of the nineteenth century. White ethnic workers also felt the loss of jobs during this time, and much of their frustration was misplaced on the Chinese sojourners.[18] In 1871, European immigrants murdered twenty-one Chinese immigrants in Los Angeles. This was one of many attacks on Chinese communities during a time of job shortages and vehement xenophobia. Chinese immigrants learned to survive by moving eastward to less antagonistic areas and by adopting occupations Europeans deemed undesirable yet appropriate for the "celestials." However, this is not to imply that the persecution of Chinese residents ended after Chinese men entered the domestic market. For instance, many Chinese laundry men were targets of racist laws that forbade the carrying of baskets hung on poles. They were also taxed heavily for each worker they employed in a laundry. In addition, laundries were the first properties destroyed during the 1877 anti-Chinese riots in San Francisco.[19]

Times were also difficult for those who ventured East to new towns. In the 1930s, sociologist Paul Siu recorded the experiences of those who arrived in Chicago. He wrote of their passage eastward:

With the completion of the railroad, the Chinese who had been building it lost their jobs. Those who did not save for a rainy day starved to death. Some began to travel toward the East. They usually traveled in small bands of several persons. They bought a hundred pound sack of rice, divided it into small sacks and each one of them carried one. On their way they cooked whenever they found wood and water. On their way they stopped to buy a pound of fat for cooking. If they had money, they could buy some meat, but if they had no money, they might take off their shoes, roll up their sleeves, and catch some fish for dinner in the pond. Then they made an earthen stove, took out the fat and began to fry the fish. Some of them finally reached Chicago. At Lake and Clark Streets they first found their lodging place. Later a store was established.[20]

How these men learned the "female" trade of laundry is a telling story of how the traits associated with a particular form of labor are reified to represent an entire race of people. A simplistic, essentialist analysis of occupations would state that certain people have a particular propensity to perform certain types of labor.[21] Siu relates one European American's impression of Chinese laundry men:

> The first impression I had of the Chinese laundryman fixed in me the conception of the hard-working, docile Oriental, capable of sly, criminal behavior if given a chance. He has been pictured, and quite correctly, as a slavelike worker, fond of working long hours for very low pay, as one who would do this in sheer gratitude to get away from the perpetual rice-and-birds'-nest diet of China.[22]

Not surprisingly, the stereotypes embedded in this passage conveniently fit the job description for laundry men. The feminized characteristics of the labor are placed upon the worker.

The fact that there were no laundries in China during the mid-1800s comes as a surprise to many who viewed Chinese, or Asians, as "born" with the "gift" to wash clothes. Siu reports that these men learned to wash and iron from church ladies in California. Such labor was performed only by women in China. However, in the United States, the economic and social changes required the men to alter their social construction of gender. The gender construction that accompanies domestic work is accepted, to some degree, as a temporary means of survival. However, the disjuncture between the gendered work and the worker contributed to xenophobic notions of "foreignness" and racist stereotypes of Chinese immigrants as sexual deviants. So-called feminine traits of passivity and submissiveness, when placed upon men who physically and culturally departed from the norm, implied a character defect.

In the beginning, these men took solace in the fact that, despite the indignities of their work, their male role as breadwinner remained intact. Their labor, alone, provided for their family in China. Siu states, "The Chinese took it as a means of survival and as a temporary job."[23] It was perhaps also comforting that other family members, particularly their wives, did not witness their form of livelihood. During their visits home, they could save face by embellishing their working conditions in the United States.

More than one hundred years later, Asian immigrants are in a similar position as domestic entrepreneurs. Interestingly, they still view small businesses as transitional mechanisms to greater mobility for the family, particularly the children.

Today, children of Asian immigrant entrepreneurs experience remnants of these xenophobic and gendered ideas. These children find themselves chafing against the long history of stereotypes pertaining to Asian Americans' labor, and their place within society. As much as they feel individual pressure for upward mobility from their immigrant parents, they also have another impetus for greater mobility into traditional white-collar professions: the desire to overcome these painful and persistent stereotypes.

Racialized Masculinity

The social construction of gender that accompanies stereotypes of Asian American entrepreneurs has had deep implications for both men's and women's gender identity. On one level, both male and female respondents report feeling suffocated by the (e)masculating and feminizing stereotypes associated with their family business, albeit in different ways. Asian American men find little or no sense of masculinity within Asian immigrant small family businesses. Stephen, a college senior, made this remark:

I've only spoken with my male friends about this . . . in some way, we're de-masculinized by being so integrated with our mothers and fathers. For me, being in this business with my mom ever since I was young and not being able to say anything, and just doing as she says, and having these people watch me follow her instructions every time, every day after school at this small jewelry store . . . it's very, very strange. No matter what kind of adult-like things I do, I'm always a child. Our lives are too integrated.

Stephen describes a sense of emasculation due to his intense involvement with his family business. Working with his mother in a subservient manner has made expressing his masculinity/adulthood difficult. Stephen, like his peers, is very conscious of what the customer—who is usually native-born and non-Asian—sees. He is aware of the stereotypes that exist and how he does or does not fit them.

Jachinson Chan, in his research on contemporary Asian American men, explains: " . . . Asian American men are given a false choice: either we emulate white American notions of masculinity or accept the fact that we are not men."[24] He adds, "Asian American masculinity, as a social construct, has been defined largely by the reproduction of stereotypes in American popular culture."[25] Given such a problematic source of gender identity, the issue of stereotypes plays an important role in Asian American men's sense of self. Ironically, they may utilize a homophobic "compulsory heterosexual model of masculinity" in an attempt to counter the initial homophobic stereotype associated with Asian males.[26]

A passage from Siu's fieldwork from the 1930s reveals the use of homophobia throughout the history of Asian immigration: "I had heard that they chased boys with a red hot iron and did all kinds of mysterious and sinister things in their back rooms."[27] This story about what allegedly happens in the backrooms of a laundry owned by a Chinese immigrant alludes to homosexuality as a form of sexual perversion, specifically pedophilia. Homophobia was used against Asian immigrant men as a way of placing them in an inferior position on the hierarchy of American manhood. David Eng notes that "the acquisition of gendered identity in liberal capitalist societies is always a racialized acquisition and that the exploitation of immigrant labor is mobilized not only through the racialization of that labor but through its sexualizing."[28] Today, Asian American men continue to feel the weight of their lowly sexual status.[29] Unfortunately, the definition of mas-

culinity has made little progress beyond the narrow confines of hetero-mas-
culinity, with its essentialist qualities: athletic, aggressive, virile, and white.
It is no wonder that many Asian American men experience "sex role strain"
after falling short of these standards and facing the false choice of either
being white or not male.[30]

For those who grow up in immigrant entrepreneurial households, sex
role strain can be particularly poignant given the long and continuing history of structural disruptions in family roles. This is evident too in the
altered relationships between siblings. For instance, Edward, a 21-year-old
Korean American male, spoke of his older brother: "My brother took care
of me. When we had the [fast food] restaurant my brother would change
my diapers when he was five years old. He would call my mom at the
restaurant crying because he didn't know to change my diapers. It's really
dear to my heart what my brother did to me. My mom was really too busy
to take care of both of us." The demands of the family business require that
traditional family roles and responsibility shift. In Edward's case, his then
5-year-old brother took on his mother's role in caring for the infant. Like
Edward, many of the respondents in this study report an intense relationship with their brothers and/or sisters that took them beyond traditional
familial divisions. Older brothers and sisters become substitute fathers and
mothers. Bob, who is four years older than his brother, told me:

> When we were younger, when I was 16 and he was 12, I was more like a
> father to my brother, often disciplining him. But as we get older, the rela-
> tionship is changing for the good. It's more brotherly, more like friends,
> not just in the sense that we can play basketball together, but he can share
> with me his concerns. We're tighter and closer. On occasion we do dis-
> agree. We argue about big and little things, me embarrassing him or me
> not approving of his friends, things like that.

Bob was uncomfortable with this earlier familial role as the father and
appreciates a more equal, less burdensome relationship as this younger
brother grows older. However, it is evident that Bob continues to perform
some variation of his father-like duties. The intensity of these sibling relationships can also create tension among the siblings. Li, a 21-year-old
Chinese American male, spoke of his older sister, whom he describes as
having "raised him":

My sister is like my mom. She's always nagging me now, always yelling at me. I wouldn't say we argue a lot, but I lose my temper quickly. She calls me, pages me, "Get home." I'm like, "Stop nagging me!" Now I do appreciate her a lot. She does do a lot for me. I have her picture. I don't tell her this. It's unsaid. One of the things later down the road when we're talking about it, I'll tell her. Right now, I won't say it. I'm stubborn.

Li's relationship with his sister resembles that between a child and parent. Like a child who chafes against parental authority and loves them at the same time, Li carries a picture of his sister, unbeknownst to her. It is the only picture in his wallet.

It is perhaps during the most difficult times that the intense connection between siblings is most clear. This was the case for Andrew and his older brother, who functioned as the intermediary between Andrew and his parents during a particularly traumatic time in their family life. He spoke of his "coming-out" experience:

> . . . Probably the most majorly traumatic thing that's happened between us was that I told them that I was gay. Pretty major. Major enough for me to leave for a year. This was the only year I wasn't at the restaurant. It was late first year and second year of college. I didn't have any money and I couldn't enroll for the next semester. I had to take a semester off. I didn't have a car. I eventually got a job, but I was not in contact with them for a little bit less than a year, and when I was, it was major arguments. It wasn't that they cut me off, because a lot of Asian culture says you would never abandon your kids, but it got to a point where I couldn't take it anymore. It was too emotionally stressful on a day-to-day basis. I needed to get out. I packed up my belongings and what little clothing I had and moved. I was living with them at the time. I packed up my stuff and left. I basically cut myself off. I didn't worry about them while I was gone. That's been the only time I haven't. I knew everything was going to be okay because my brother stepped in. It was the year before he moved out of state. I kept in contact with him. When he got a job offer out of state, he called me and said, "I got this job offer. I'm taking it. They want you to come back." It was really hard. The day that I came back my dad hugged me, which was absolutely unheard of. Since then we don't really talk about it, that whole year, which is fine but I really wish they would. That's their issue.

Andrew came back home with the understanding that his parents needed one of the two children to help out at their small Chinese restaurant; there were no other employees. He did so because he understood that his older brother had done his part and now it was his responsibility to help with the family business. While Andrew would like a more open and communicative relationship with his parents, he understands their silence as a normal part of their "don't ask, don't tell" relationship. Instead, Andrew works a second job during the day at an AIDS advocacy center and then goes to the family restaurant each evening. His homosexuality—an important part of Andrew's identity—is left unspoken.

Racialized Femininity

For Asian American women, the stereotypes associated with Asian immigrant labor are also constricting. While masculinity is neglected in this stereotype, a particular, racialized, form of femininity is strictly enforced. According to Karen Pyke and Denise Johnson, "Asian American and white American women serve . . . as uniform categorical representations of the opposing forces of female oppression and egalitarianism."[31] The feminine stereotype associated with Asian immigrant labor constricts Asian American women within an orientalist construction that presents them, once again, as exotic and strange. Within this racial and gendered arena, being a woman implies servitude. One student I interviewed, Carrie, talked about the pressures she felt to behave like a "proper waitress" at her family's restaurant:

> I have never played the docile, subservient Asian girl crap at home or anywhere so I try to act the same at the restaurant. My parents have gotten to realize that I will never be their model, ideal daughter and I think they have accepted me for who I am. I'm not sure if they just gave up or are proud of me . . . I can never define the boundaries between the two concepts.

The familial pressures to be a "good daughter" are reinforced by the business pressures to be a "good servant." Carrie and her female peers are conscious of the stereotypes of Asian American women and react strongly to them. They experience a paradox in which they feel the need both to excel (or dominate) as an individual and to be submissive as a woman at the family business. This paradox is particularly poignant in their relationships with their mothers. Most of these young women witnessed the transformation of their mothers from homemaker or pink-collar worker to business partner. The mothers in these households report having substantial decision-making power within the home as well as at work.[32] The mothers represent contemporary superwomen who work outside the home and raise a family.

However, the second generation women continue to feel pressure to behave like a "proper Asian girl" from a variety of sources, including their mothers. Like Asian American men, Asian American women also experience sex role strain. It is apparent that their gender identity construction is a work in progress and that popular images of Asians dating back to the 1800s continue to play a large role in their lives.

Given the dramatic transformations in work and family roles of Asian immigrant entrepreneurial households, it seems counter-intuitive to find traditional hierarchical structures maintained among family members. However, this is the case for the families I interviewed. In fact, the respondents attempt to minimize the disruptions in traditional work and family roles by applying traditional expectations of gender on the type of work performed by a female versus a male. For instance, Trinh, the oldest of four children, said: "My brothers are busboys. They do the harder, more difficult 'manly' tasks. I'm the waitress. Whenever a group of guys comes into the restaurant, [my mom] would tell me to wait on them and act 'friendly' [laughs]." Her statement contradicts my observations at her family's Chinese and Vietnamese restaurant. First, Trinh worked significantly more hours than both of her brothers combined. Second, Trinh worked just as hard as, if not harder than, her brothers. This was true during each of my unannounced visits to the restaurant. Third, I observed Trinh also bussing tables but never witnessed her brothers waiting on tables.

This unequal social construction of difference is common in communities that have experienced a traumatic or significant social change. The maintenance of traditional family roles is an effort to "normalize" a disruption in the social fabric. For instance, in August Hollingshead's classic study *Elmtown's Youth*, he describes how the Great Depression blurred the boundaries of gender and class in one American town.[33] To compensate, the town created an elaborate system of age segregation. The system "sought to ensure 'proper' development by separating youth from the adult world of their parents."[34] Gender is socially constructed through a deliberate separation of mutually exclusive roles,[35] and these mutually exclusive categories become particularly important in times of change. It is not surprising, then, that when men become unemployed, they perform even less housework than they did when they were employed.[36] Since work is men's main source of identity, the absence of work is traumatic to their sense of masculinity.[37] Consequently, performing "women's work" during this time further exacerbates their insecurities. This insecurity reinforces the need for traditional, patriarchal divisions of labor.

Everybody's Kung Fu Fighting

In the 1970s, *Kung Fu* was a popular television series starring David Carradine.[38] The story followed a basic Western narrative, but this time, the main character was a half Chinese, half (white) American Shaolin priest and Kung Fu expert named Kwai Chang Caine. Caine was a loner who drifts from town to town throughout the American West in search of his half-brother. Caine, played by a white American, David Carradine, does not properly function to normalize the experiences of Asian Americans. In fact, the "foreignness" of the lead character is intensified against the American backdrop of the Western frontier. Bruce Lee, the talented Chinese American actor and martial arts expert, was originally considered for this part. However, he was rejected by the studio as "too Chinese." Vijay Prashad writes, "The dismissal sent Bruce packing to Hong Kong and into history. *Kung Fu*, on the other hand, became all that Bruce disavowed. Set in the nineteenth century, the show has Caine (half Chinese, half white) taking on racism by his own individual, superhuman initiative; other Asians appear passive or as memories of a grand era long past and always exotic."[39] After years of travel, as the series ends Caine never settles down in the United States. A Chinese American hero played by an actual Chinese American who knows that he/she is Chinese American could not exist then, and this remains a challenge still today.

However, the pursuit of heroes as embodied in these Western narratives continues to occupy the everyday lives of second generation Asian Americans. Asian American heroes who star in immigrant narratives represent a "normal" picture of American life. In this way, these children are like *all* American children. Their unique familial experiences growing up in a small family business—with its premature adulthood, prolonged childhood, and lack of boundaries between work and family—are captured in a common American tale of heroes, enduring struggles, and happy endings. The fact that persistent business failure does not imply parental failure is a strong testament to the power of their narratives.

The next chapter extends this discussion by focusing on the implications of this immigrant narrative on the children's sense of obligation to their parents. Unlike native-born entrepreneurs, the immigrant small family business is merely a tool of mobility. Asian immigrant children are generally expected to move beyond the family business. These children report pressure from their parents to go into "stable," well-paying, and most important, status-laden professions such as medicine and law. Apparently, it is not so impressive to tell the neighbors that your child decided to become a sociologist.

CHAPTER SIX

Consumption Fantasies of Upward Mobility

> After seeing the sacrifices that my parents have made, I am motivated to maximize my future earnings potential and build a successful career. Let's be honest. I don't have a trust fund and my parents have invested a lot of time, money, and debt into my education. I can't afford to be an English major. My parents have never told me to be a lawyer or be rich. However, after seeing my parents work forty–plus hours a week for years, I have internalized a deep motivation to be successful.
>
> —Richard, 20, Korean American

Upward Mobility as Conspicuous Consumption

Richard's family owns a general merchandise store that sells T-shirts and other tourist-oriented trinkets. In his interview, he expresses an unspoken understanding between him and his parents. They never came out and told him what he could or could not be "when he grew up," but their expectations were clear. They did not have to say a word—instead, Richard stood alongside his father and mother during those seemingly endless days at the store restocking shelves and watched as they worked the counter politely serving even the rudest of customers. As a young boy, Richard remembers how tired he felt sitting on a stool next to the cash register, sweating from the summer heat that poured through the glass doors. He kept his complaints to a minimum because he knew that his parents were more fatigued than he.

When asked if he intended to take over his family's store, Richard responded, "No, I plan on being a professional. I'm going to law school." Richard is not alone in his intended pattern of mobility, understanding of success, and deep sense of obligation to his parents. On the whole, the adolescents and young adults in this study are decisive, practical people. When asked what they wanted to do with their life, each had a ready answer. Almost every respondent aspired to be a professional of some sort, mostly in law, medicine, or business (related to finance or computers). Like his peers, Charlie views himself as an extension of his immigrant parents' dream of upward mobility in the United States. He is determined to elevate his parents' social status through the conspicuous consumption associated with his career choice.

However decisive they appear in their career decisions, many respondents also underwent some internal conflict during the process of making their decision. This was particularly clear of the younger respondents. During an interview with a focus group of second generation high school students, each respondent answered the question "What do you want to do in the future?" using a similar pattern. Each began by saying, "What I *like* to do is ———, but what I'm *going* to do is _____." For instance, 15-year-old Janice said, "What I like to do is paint and draw, but I'm going to be an accountant." Similarly, Han, a 16-year-old Chinese American, said, "I really like to write short stories and stuff, but I've decided to go into computers 'cause that's the future."

The second generation feels the pressure of representing the success or failure of immigrant "adaptation" in the United States. Therefore, upward economic mobility is a central theme in these children's lives. Career decisions are perhaps the most prominent form of conspicuously displayed consumption. This pursuit of greater social status is ultimately a pursuit of legitimate social citizenship. For the children of immigrant entrepreneurs, the business itself is a tool of mobility. The business—and, by extension, work—is seen as a necessary burden or sacrifice that must be endured for the sake of greater familial economic mobility. The second generation negotiates various obligations, expectations, and sacrifices in order to build the social capital necessary to ensure upward mobility not only for themselves but also for the first generation. By displaying evidence of attaining the American Dream, they hope to be finally be treated as the Americans that they are.

This chapter focuses on the issue of upward mobility through the conspicuous consumption of their career choices. To do this, I investigate the children's definitions of success and failure, their perception of happiness, and their sense of obligation to their parents as they plan their future. I illustrate how the pursuit of upward mobility through conspicuous consumption affects the daily decisions of these second generation Asian Americans, particularly during the tumultuous stage of young adulthood. This issue is significant in understanding not only why second generation Asian Americans make certain career choices, but also what are some of the potential social costs of making them. It is apparent that these decisions are made through a difficult process involving a careful consideration of the obligations and expectations of their parents and the demands of the American Dream.

Redefining Success and Failure

For many children of immigrant entrepreneurs, career success has very little to do with happiness. The road to success is a narrow one, paved with hard work and monetary gains rather than a sense of emotional fulfillment, enjoyment, or happiness. This definition of success was evident throughout the interviews. As one student put it, "The primary purpose of working is to support the family not to enjoy the work." Likewise, Jane said, "They wouldn't do this business out of fun. Everything is for us. Maybe that's why we feel such an obligation. They would never have entered into this if they didn't think they should build something for us."

When asked whether they felt the family business was a success, most answered in the positive. However, it was not a simple yes or no answer. They qualified their answer by defining what they viewed as a success. This qualification was necessary to distance the parents from any business failure (and to ensure the heroic status of the father, as discussed in the previous chapter). This imposed boundary between work and family outcomes is necessary for these children, who feel the need to defend or protect the image of their parents as good, successful immigrants. By making this separation, the child is able to maintain his or her role as a good, filial son or daughter and deflect any attribution of failure away from the parents. Those who do not impose this boundary tend to have a more strained relationship with their parents. Therefore, the question of whether or not the family business is a success was difficult to answer. Given the complexities behind the answer, many respondents felt the need to redefine success and failure to justify their response. For example, one interviewee described his family's business as a "partial success." He explained:

> On one level, the business is a success because obviously my parents have enough money to put me through college and they have the resources to support our whole family with a comfortable standard of living. However, it's a partial success in terms of quality of life. I mean that in order to maintain this standard of living, it requires a lot of time and effort by my parents. . . . [T]hey are no better off than when they started the business years ago.

The business was a success for providing material gain and human capital for the second generation, but the cost to do so was significant. The entire family, particularly the parents, had to give up the "quality" or kind of life they would rather have.

Charlie responded in this way: "Hmmmmm . . . I guess it is considered a success because it was able to provide my tuition, family car, home, and all the necessities and luxuries as well." However, if greater mobility for the first generation is included in this equation, most immigrant small family businesses would be considered failures. Instead, the focus is on the material goods necessary for attainment of greater social status for the second generation. Another respondent, Kyung Ah, also struggled with this dichotomy. When asked if she thought her family's business was a success or failure, she replied:

> Wow. Those are really hard things to attach to the business because it was a success in that it supported our family for about fifteen years. In the end it was really struggling. My parents would probably say that it was a failure because they didn't get to retire or build up their nest egg or anything like that. I'm proud that they had the store. I'm proud that they did what they wanted to. . . . My brother, my sister and I all went on to get advanced degrees . . . . Personally, I would consider it a success because it supported the family.

It is evident that many of these businesses would not be considered a success in the conventional sense—the financial bottom line. In fact, most respondents experienced the loss of more than one business due to lack of profits. Ordinarily, this would be considered a failure. However, these children re-define failure as success by drawing on and prioritizing familial indicators. In Kyung Ah's case, she viewed the business as a success in light of her and her siblings' educational and career outcomes.

The redefinition of the business as a success also suggests a sense of filial piety on the part of children. For instance, Maria said this about her family's take-out restaurant: "It's a success in terms of customers coming back because they recognize my dad. My dad has this really weird personality and I think they are attracted to that." Maria presents her father as a success, and subsequently defines the restaurant as a success. She went on to add: "I admire my dad. He's so cool. But also they didn't expect as much success as they have now. So, I think we're kind of lucky. It's not the best business in the world but we're doing pretty well." Most respondents, mindful of the need to respect their elders, draw a distinction between the business and the parents when businesses fail. Even those who describe the business as a failure are careful not to blame their parents. Alice, a Korean American college junior, described her family's dry-cleaning business as a failure. She explained, "I'm talking financially, of course. The business makes a small profit of about $45,000 a year, which is very little in view of how many hours my parents work—about twelve to fourteen hours a day, six days a week." Here, Alice notes how hard her parents work and the inadequate reward for their labor. She is also clear in her definition of failure as strictly financial—"of course," she said—lest the reader venture to make assumptions past the boundary of work and into her family.

However, a few respondents (n = 6) did not make this distinction between the failure of the business and the failure of their parents. For them, the business is clearly defined as a failure, and the outcome is attributed to the parents. This is the case with Beth, a Chinese American college freshman, who described her family's Chinese restaurant as a financial failure. She does not separate work from family and instead places the blame squarely upon her parents: "It's not succeeding. I wouldn't say it's succeeding. It's just a means of making a living. It's just to get by day by day." She then discussed what she thought the problem was: "It's just at a standstill. The business isn't doing as well . . . they're not running it as strictly business; it's more like family. Just, you know, open for the family. They've got like a TV in the front and they're sitting there watching it and whatnot." Beth's definition of success differs from that of her peers. To her, simply making a living does not equal even partial success. Much to her chagrin, her parents have transformed the "front" of the restaurant, which is generally reserved as the customers' space, into their living room. She explained that the customers feel uncomfortable, as if they had intruded into a stranger's home and imposed upon them. Ironically, Beth blames her parents' lack of professionalism or boundaries between family and work for the business failure. It is also evident that she is frustrated with her parents' lack of upward mobility. From her perspective, her parents have not lived up to their responsibility to unselfishly provide a promising future. Interestingly, Beth described herself as working class. She is one of only four entrepreneurial respondents in the study who reported a family income level below "middle class."[1]

Susan, another Chinese American college freshman, also deemed her parents a failure. In her case, Susan consciously rejected both her parents and the family restaurant. She was unable, at the time, to reinterpret her parents' long hours at the family restaurant as a sacrifice made on her behalf. She continues to feel neglected and angry. It is evident that the boundary work[2] of separating work from home life is, at times, a difficult endeavor.

The Insignificance of Happiness

In the pursuit of success, happiness has little place. Bob's father owned a tool shop in Los Angeles. After the Los Angeles riots/unrest in 1992, they lost the shop through bankruptcy. A year later the father started a new business painting houses. Bob helps his father on his jobs and assessed the new business in this way: "I consider it a success, even though it's still in its first year. It's doing well. I don't think he really enjoys what he does, but he understands that he makes good money. It's what he knows how to do. He just does it."

Happiness is a contentious and elusive issue. Second generation children experience strong pressures to continue their parents' upward mobility trajectory. And as the children have discovered, happiness has little to do with upward movement. In fact, the children's pursuit of their own individual happiness may slow down or stop their parents' goal of intergenerational

TABLE 6.1
Parents' Satisfaction and Happiness with Work*

Response	Satisfied (%)	Happy (%)
Yes	39	21
Somewhat yes	34	20
No	27	59
Total	100	100

*Respondents were asked, "Are your parents satisfied and/or happy working at the family business?"

upward mobility. They do the best job they can regardless of whether or not the work provides happiness in their lives. As Bob says, "I just do it."

In their interviews, each respondent was asked, "Do you think your parents are satisfied or happy with what they do?" Many respondents made a distinction between the two concepts. For example, Maria said, "I don't think they're a hundred percent satisfied, but they are satisfied—but not happy. They complain about how hard it is. My mom complains about work all the time." The respondents define satisfaction as a sense of accomplishment and happiness as a sense of joy. This distinction implies that even through one may perform one's job well, the job itself is limited in providing enjoyment. There is a sense of under-employment in which the parent's potential is under-utilized. In this scenario, the parents do all they can, but it is the work/labor that is not satisfactory.

Whereas almost 73 percent of my sample described their parents as satisfied or somewhat satisfied, only 41 percent described their parents as happy or somewhat happy with their form of employment (see Table 6.1). The respondents generally qualified their answers, as illustrated by Tony, whose family owns a smoke shop in the San Francisco Bay Area: "We're doing a lot better than we did [before]. I think my mom is happy that we're doing well, in a sense, but kind of not happy in that it is seven days a week fourteen hours a day, and there isn't really time for anything else. You go to work. But it's a lot better than when we were broke."

The respondents listed hard manual labor, low status and prestige, lack of "quality time," and rude customers as the four biggest impediments to happiness at work. For instance, after describing the family business as a success, Tony said, "My parents are definitely not happy. It's physically draining, and emotionally stressful dealing with customers." Likewise, Charlie said that his parents "would be happier if they were able to cut back on the workload and spend more time pursuing hobbies or spending time with the family or just relaxing." The children distance the manual labor of their family business from the identity of their parents. Laura said this: " . . . [M]y dad has mentioned that he would have been good at something else. They're not saying, 'This is my life calling.'"

This sense of a "calling" implies a moral or higher sense of duty driven by a deeper motivation or connection to one's labor. In accordance with the heroic immigrant narrative, second generation Asian Americans redefine their parents' work as evidence of a deeper motivation—as a form of sacrifice on their behalf. For instance, Bob said this about his parents:

> Their number one priority is for my education and my future goals, as well as my brother's. There's a Korean phrase that says that their generation is constantly bending over—if you imagine a plant, my brother and I are budding and they're drying up the sun. As a result of that, their first priority is to provide for us to be successful and do whatever we want.

The often humble, stereotypical, stance that their parents exhibit when serving (American) customers is perceived as not evidence of the parents' "true self," but rather a fictive performance endured as a necessary parental sacrifice. The business is clearly a stepping-stone. Jin, for instance, spoke of his mother's struggle to deal with her sense of worth while working at the family's diner:

> My mom hates the restaurant business. She enjoys making customers happy, but she came from an educated background. She was the only girl in her family. Her father was very educated. She was one of the few women in her community who was sent to school. She was one of the few women in her community who was sent to school. Her father wanted her to study even though women didn't do it at that time. She always wanted to study. She put her work ethic into me: "You don't want to be flipping burgers and standing twelve hours a day." She would cry sometimes. She would fight with my dad.

He went on to add: "She took all the earnings they made in one day and threw it into the ocean. She didn't think America was going to be so much work. *I always said I was going to live her dreams for her.* Now she gets up at 4:30 in the morning and studies English, does her homework. That's a good thing." Through sheer frustration, Jin's mother threw away their hard earned money. Her actions could be interpreted as a symbolic rejection—if only for a day—of being relegated to the lowly status of a worker/laborer. The act of sending the day's earnings into the ocean, where its value is rendered meaningless, signifies her claim that she is more than her job and that the person her customers encounter is not the real her—that she is in fact more than her role in this site of consumption.

There is a sense of a deeper calling that has been lost for Jin's mother. Jin is unusual and perhaps even lucky to be one of the few children who are privy to this narrative of personal shame and melancholy expressed by his mother. In Jin's eyes, his mother is stronger for showing her pain, and for striving for something greater. Jin's sense of obligation to his mother, then, is as dramatic as his mother's sense of loss. He believes he must fill the melancholic void felt by his parents. As he told me later: "How can I not?"

This incident also illustrates the traumatic experience of downward mobility that is common among highly educated Asian immigrants who find themselves underemployed after migration to the United States. Money alone does not bring happiness. Sky, whose family owns two dry-cleaning businesses in a suburb of a large metropolitan city, told me, "Financially, it's very, very successful. But emotionally and physically, not at all." Rather, money must be accompanied by high social status, stability, and respect. Beth had a similar explanation to Jin's for why her parents continuously pressure her and her younger sister to strive for more: "No pension, health insurance, benefits . . . stuff like that. And [my mom] would have more time at home and stuff instead of always being at the restaurant. And my dad, I think he had more in mind, because he's always pushing us to do better. He probably thought he could do better or would like to do better." Financially successful or not, these children of immigrants express an obligation to pay off their "debts." I asked Alice, who described her parents as unhappy with their working conditions, what would make them happy with what they did. She replied: "My parents are happy people. They are the happiest they could expect, considering that they aren't using their talents and abilities to their fullest. . . . But they used to have regrets, about not doing what they really wanted to do in life. My dad has a M.D. from Korea and my mom majored in art at Seoul University. They have very little time to do what interests them."

As part of this upward mobility project, the children do not intend to take over the family business. In this case, the business is merely a temporary stepping stone for more mainstream status-laden endeavors. Understandably then, the parents do not expect their children to follow in their footsteps. This picture differs from Herbert Gans's general interpretation of immigrant children as so overwhelmed by a youth culture and the freedoms unavailable in their old country that they become unwilling to accept immigrant parental work norms or to work in "un-American" conditions, as many of their parents do.[3] Rather, the Asian American second generation is *not allowed* to accept the working conditions of their parents. To do so would defeat the parents' purpose for working as hard as they have. Social mobility would be stunted should the child decide to continue working at the family business.

The working conditions and social implications of immigrant self-employment make the family business a difficult place to work in. The small family business, for these respondents, represents a dream deferred. The sense of sacrifice by the parents presents a significant burden and obligation on the children to make up for the parents' loss.

Repayment Obligations

Each respondent expressed a need to "repay" his or her parents in some way (see Table 6.2). Underlying these feelings is an assumption that their parents willingly stunted their own growth so that their children would prosper and that it is solely the childrens' responsibility to compensate for their loss.

The respondents describe three distinct forms of repayment: (1) to offer a token of their gratitude; (2) to demonstrate their own success in education and financial wealth; and (3) to provide for their parents' retirement. The common trait shared by all three, however, is that they are conspicu-

TABLE 6.2
Sense of Obligation to Repay Parents*

Respondents	Yes	No	Total
Entrepreneurial	69 (97%)	2 (3%)	71
Non-entrepreneurial	15 (88%)	2 (12%)	17

*Respondents were asked, "Do you feel a sense of obligation to repay your parents?"

ously status-laden. The most obvious form is the first, giving a token of gratitude, which is usually in the form of expensive consumer goods. Luxury cars and homes are the most popular material goods cited. For Maria, it is a brand new black Lexus LS for her parents. For Beth, it is a Cadillac for her father. For Bob, it is a Mercedes-Benz. For Jennifer, it is a BMW and a house next door. Sage, a 22-year-old Chinese American, was about to graduate from her university and had already accepted a position with a high-tech corporation in Silicon Valley. She has high hopes of how she will repay her parents. She said, "My signing bonus, I gave it to my mother. Whatever extra income—bonus money—I don't need, I'm going to give to them for the next two years. After that, hopefully, I'll be able to buy them a car and then buy them a house."

A less obvious form of repayment is the career success of the second generation and it usually follows the respondent's initial thoughts of fancy automobiles and other material goods. For example, Bob told me:

> I always feel an obligation to repay my parents. At first I thought it would come in the form of a Mercedes-Benz, but more and more I'm realizing that it's more of filial piety and more like a loyalty kind of thing, not so much financial things. I could send [my dad] a $500 check every month and not talk with him for the rest of my life. [But, it's] not just monetary, but being their son and providing for them.

Like his peers, Bob went from purely financially driven modes of repayment to include a sense of filial piety. Driving around a luxury car purchased by a son or daughter is more meaningful when the car is a token of the child's larger success. What is significant is the status of the career path the good son/daughter has chosen. Edward related feeling this pressure in high school when choosing which college to attend:

> They actually wanted me to go to Stanford. They know the big-name schools. Their standard is you've got to go to Stanford or something. Choosing my college was up to me. In the end they were happy about it. They asked friends and people if they had heard of Dartmouth. The lawyer that I spoke to is a member of our church. He was like, "Yeah, that's a very good school." Once he said that, it was like, he knows what he's talking about.

For Edward's parents, the brand-name status of particular schools was one of the only ways to evaluate the quality of a university. His parents clearly understood that by attending a "famous" institution, their child would have greater access to the status and subsequent privileges of higher income, stability, and social citizenship. This is the American Dream. However, not everyone was comfortable with this pressure. Jin, a Korean American college senior, found himself overwhelmed. He said,

> My parents have my future set out for me, who I should marry, what kind of school I should be going to. I hate that. Overly concerned about how other people live. Who cares about what other people do? You've got to find your own niche. Money is very important. It's not everything, but it's important. I'm uncomfortable when they like to advertise or show off my success in front of other people.

Jin feels a sense of obligation toward his parents and is, in fact, well on his way to fulfilling those expectations through his upcoming graduation from a prestigious university, where he earned high grades. Even so, he is unsettled by his role as a poster-boy for immigrant success.

Li, on the other hand, has no problems conforming to his parents' expectations. As the third and last child in the family, he has taken on the rather grand role as the favorite son and last hope. This is how describes his place in the family:

> I think I play a key a role in the family. My brother married white, an Italian. I wouldn't say they're embarrassed, but they're not too pleased. My dad is very traditional. He likes to show off anything. The fact that his elder son married a non-Asian, he's not able to show it off. My sister is going to be in someone else's family when she marries. I'm the only one left to succeed, marry Asian, and give my dad points over his friends so he

can show off. All the pressure falls on me. . . . When we were kids, my grandma would always mutter to me and say, "You have to marry Asian, you have to marry Chinese." They totally blew up when my brother said he was going to marry an Italian. Then my grandma said, "Don't be like your older brother." My grandma says, "Marry Asian. I will give you so much money. I'll give you my whole house, everything." They all love me. My mom doesn't speak English at all, and I want my wife and kids to be able to communicate with her. That's the hard part when we have dinner, my brother, his wife can't communicate with them. Someone tells a joke and everyone's laughing and Justine's sitting there. Someone has to translate. By then everyone has lost it. The translation is not even funny. She says, "I dread coming to family dinners just because I don't understand." I don't want to have that happen with my family. I want them to feel comfortable. Communication is one of the biggest issues I have to deal with. That's one reason I want to marry Chinese.

Li feels the need to compensate for the actions of his older brother. He also has an older sister, who is largely left out of the picture due to her gender. Li explained that she married into another family and consequently is out of their family. This traditional notion of gender expectation is also common in discussions of parental retirement—the third form of repayment.

Regardless of the fact that both men and women expressed this sense of obligation and the same three general forms of repayment, there is a distinctly gendered understanding of their actions. For men, their responses are remarkable for their invocation of the gendered role of the male breadwinner and the cultural role of the dutiful son. For instance, Edward explained: "Yes, I do feel an obligation to repay them. Not necessarily in terms of dollar-for-dollar. . . . I'll provide whatever they need and try to be a dutiful son." Barney, another Korean American male, said, "I feel an obligation to repay my parents by finishing school faster so I can hurry up and get on with my career so they can retire." Similarly, Charlie explained why he wanted to repay his parents: "I think the best decision my parents made was to come to the U.S. I've been to Korea and Korea sucks. I think that my living standard is better than any of my "rich" relatives in Korea. My parents have worked and sacrificed a lot. I will pay them back by hopefully providing for their retirement."

By visiting his parents' home country, Charlie had a view of what his life could have been. This insight helped instill in him a sense of gratitude towards his parents. Similar to the other respondents, Charlie's feelings of indebtedness grew gradually. Any expectations on the parents' part were largely unspoken. For instance, Ben explained that he did not feel pressured to succeed or care for his family, but that it was something he wanted to do. Ben intends to give his parents the upward mobility they had postponed. In fact, Ben has already "selected" the plot of land in Westchester County, New York, where he would like to build a four-bedroom house with a three-car garage. Half-jokingly, Ben replied that he had already chosen the make and color of the three automobiles that will inhabit each of the garage spaces. Jack expressed similar thoughts. He did not view his caretaker role as an obligation at all, but rather as a taken-for-granted cultural expectation. "I'll probably end up repaying them when they get older," he said. "Asian families are like that. We're always close and we take care of our own parents. It's just like that."

The women in the sample also expressed a desire to care for their parents during their retirement. On the whole, the women's responses combine both traditional gender roles and a more contemporary sense of individual accomplishment. For example, Kyung Ah, the youngest of three children, discussed her parent's retirement: "As my parents get older, my brother will be caring for them financially and my sister and I will help out too." She and her sister expect to provide emotional support for her parents while her oldest brother provides financial assistance. Those women who feel a financial obligation, in addition to emotional nurturance, alluded to this gender-bending role as a point of pride. Jennifer, for instance, told me: "It's usually the boy that's supposed to take care of the parents. But my parents are expecting me to take care of them. They're like, we're living with you. When you buy a house, we're moving in." Likewise, Sky explained, "I think I play the hope for my parents. I feel like I need to be a big success because they're losing hope in my brother. It's like, 'Please show us that we didn't completely mess up with childrearing.' I'm the light at the end of the tunnel. It's gotta happen. They know how strong I am. I'm definitely the individualist, not the traditional girl." Like Li, Sky feels she must make up for the shortcomings of her sibling. Being more like a son, in this case, is a compliment and a sign of her parent's confidence in her.

There are other circumstances in which women perform the son's role. For Jane, it is the death of her father nine years ago and the fact that she is the oldest of three girls. She noted, "I plan to care for my mother financially after I am finished with my education. Since I'm the oldest of a family of three girls, I think I've played a son's role in my family."

Given that the parents' labor is seen as simply a means to facilitate the children's mobility, many respondents presented their parents' retirement as coinciding with their own college graduation. This is particularly true for the adolescents in the study, whose parents are years from retirement and who are perhaps less realistic. One respondent, Jiang, said: "Right when I graduate, they're selling it. My dad might work weekends just to keep his hands busy. He likes to work but working twelve hours a day is just too much." Frequently the children of immigrants appear to have fairly romantic notions of their parents' retirement. It is viewed as a momentous occasion for their parents, who will finally get the chance to relax and enjoy life. It is also a momentous occasion in the children's lives, as they view retirement as the end of a source of burden and sacrifice. Upon retirement, their parents will no longer have a business and thus can no longer accrue points of obligation from it. (However, the repayment schedule may continue to be just as grueling.)

When asked if her parents had any specific plans after she finished school, another interviewee said: "They want to retire. They're like, 'As soon as you get out of school, we're retiring. We're selling the business.' I don't know if or when they'll sell the place. My dad always talks about retirement. He just likes talking about it." It appears that talking about retirement is also a form of wishful thinking on the parents' part. This is the case for Robert, whose parents have an unusually fertile imagination. He describes his parents' detailed plan for upward mobility:

They talk about [retirement] in a way that scares me out of my mind. What's supposed to happen is I'm supposed to marry a childhood friend of mine and my mom is best friends with her mom. [My mom] has known this woman (friend's daughter) since she was born basically. We've had contact but there's no sort of feeling whatsoever, I think. Well, I think she may have some sort of feelings for me but I don't, but she doesn't seem to care because her mom is even more dominating than mine. So, that's part of the problem. And then they're going to sell this house and then put a down payment on a very large house somewhere else, way far away, because then they won't have to commute because they would be retired or something like that. It will be a huge house so that, quote, "Us young kids could have our own privacy but we'll all be living together."

Robert describes his parents' planning process as their "vacation." He adds, "I just want them to leave me out of it." Robert's parents' view of retirement is at odds with what it means for their children.

The respondents look forward to their parents' retirement as a time when the intense family ties will loosen. With the absence of the business, the children expect a new phase in their lives. In a sense, the obligations will stop accruing and the children will find a moment to breathe before starting their repayments. In Robert's case, however, his parents plan to cash in their chips immediately and not to loosen their connections with their only son.

Preparing for the Future

These obligations and expectations are forms of familial social capital that help bring about intergenerational upward mobility. They are factors that help formulate a normative structure of mobility. However, these factors must be embedded within strong social ties to ensure repayment. Family ties are, along with religious and community ties, important in forming a "closed" social network[4] that leads family members to act selflessly in "the family's" interest and can level sanctions against those who resist internalizing these norms.

Social capital is understood as a fragile phenomenon. Different social contexts produce different normative structures. Therefore, the strict social networks created by immigrant parents and the ethnic community may weaken as children move away to college and become exposed to new social structures with greater rewards or sanctions. It is logical to assume that once a student is away at college and distances himself or herself from his/her intense involvement with and obligations to the family and the family business, s/he would develop alternative goals, and other career paths.

However, this was not the case for the respondents interviewed for this study. No matter how far the children moved away from the family and however slight their involvement with the family store, their expectation to repay their parents remained as strong as ever. This was true for both the

TABLE 6.3
Career Choices of Children of Immigrants[1]

Career Choices	Entrepreneurial (n=71)	Non-entrepreneurial (n=17)
Standard professions[2]	57 (80%)	11 (65%)
Non-standard professions[3]	11 (15%)	2 (12%)
Undecided	3 (4%)	4 (24%)

[1] Respondents were asked, "What do you want to do as a career?"
[2] The majority identified business, medicine, or law. In addition, there were one of each: architect, journalist, and professor.
[3] These professions included: actress, event planner, social worker, teacher, writer, missionary, and musician.

entrepreneurial and non-entrepreneurial sample. Table 6.3 outlines the breakdown of the interviewees' career choices.

The vast majority of those interviewed had clear notions about their career trajectory following college graduation.[5] Traditional professions that are status-laden and associated with high income were their primary choices, particularly for those from entrepreneurial households. When they discussed the motivations for their choices, their parents' (unspoken) expectations and sense of obligation weighed heavily. Dean, an 18-year-old Korean American college freshman, spoke of why he was currently majoring in biology with the hope of entering medical school upon graduation: "I often thought that it might be more my parents' idea, me getting into med school, than my idea. But I understand that they're looking out for me. They want me to have a great source of income. I know everything they do is in my best interest. They're happy about my decision."

The presence of parents was also evident in Kristen's interview. Kristen is double majoring in education and marketing. She told me: "My parents have always said, 'Whatever you want to do, you can tell me and I'll support you.' My grandma, on the other hand, would rather that I did marketing or economics. I see how my dad is, how hard it is to work at the store, and how he's so tired. I told myself that I don't want that type of life." Despite the fact that she is away at college, the experiences of working alongside her father at the family store stays with her. She has decided to try two different tracks at once to fulfill both her family's wishes and her personal goals. For those with strong inclinations toward a non-traditional profession, this is an important strategy. John, whose parents own a Korean grocery store, employed this tactic so that one career choice could function as a safety-net for the other, more personal choice. He did so in large part to relieve parental fears about his future. He made it clear to his parents that he "feels an obligation to be someone successful and support them so they don't have to work anymore." John explained:

> I hope to finish [college] in another year and a half and go to cooking school on the East Coast. My parents never figured I was serious, you know. They just thought I could make a pretty good steak. But, I like working with computers too. I thought I would major in MIS (Managing Information Strategies) and if cooking doesn't work out I can go from there. As a kid I thought cooking was a lot of fun, creative, an arts and crafts kind of thing. And you get to eat it afterwards. That's the best part.

Relieving parental fears about their children's future financial security can be a difficult task for those who commit to a single career track. As Julie explains, "My dad is scared. He's a typical Asian parent, where you're supposed to be an engineer and a doctor, not a teacher, where the salary isn't that great." Judy, whose family owns a dry-cleaning business, also experienced some difficult moments when she announced to her parents last year that she intended to major in sociology. She said:

> My parents were really upset that I decided to become a sociology major. They don't really understand what it is and they think . . . they think sociology equals social worker. They want me to go to law school. Actually, [during our] last holiday break, my dad yelled at me for a long time and said that I'm basically ruining my life. If I go to law school, he'll take back everything he said. They're pretty much expecting me to go to law school. I think it's the whole prestige thing. All my older cousins—three out of four became doctors. So, I feel like a reject [laughter].

The fact that she plans to become a professor, a status-laden profession, is not enough to alleviate her parents' disappointment. Describing your daughter or son as a sociologist does not carry the prestige of an attorney or medical doctor. The parents' return on their investment diminishes as the child strays from the normative structures of an immigrant community.

As Judy's case illustrates, there is a downside to this goal of upward mobility. The path to the American Dream is a narrow one that does not allow the second generation to explore alternative goals that may provide a greater chance of happiness, personal fulfillment, or sense of belonging. Instead, there is little room for creativity or innovation, and one has to contemplate the possibilities that are lost by such narrow, socially condoned career choices. Another downside is the enormous sense of burden that individuals experience in trying to compensate for their parents' loss in social status. The costs of barriers to upward mobility, and the accompanying lack of family time, leisure, medical benefits, and respect that the parents experience, are shouldered by the children alone. The larger social structure that maintains these barriers is overlooked within this individual perspective of "responsibility." The valuable contribution that immigrants and their children make to not only the national economy but also the political ideology of the American Dream is made invisible as immigrants and their children are made to constantly justify, if not apologize for, their own presence.

Edward is in his third year at a prestigious university, and the question of what to do after graduation has been weighing heavily on him. He is an Asian studies major and has been struggling with various, contradictory expectations and obligations. He began by stating:

> I have that burden of being the first son. My parents came to America. They work hard. I got to go to school and that's going to present a lot of opportunities for me. Now I have to do my best in terms of having responsibilities to my parents and all those around me who have been supportive. If I can help it, I would like to work without having to think about money. I would like to really do something that I feel is constructive.

Given that Edward had no interest in medicine or business, he is now contemplating law. He says that he knows his parents would be happy if he went to law school, but his true passion is obvious as he excitedly discusses why he chose to major in Asian studies: "It's not going to be really something that I'm going to pursue after graduation, but I chose to study it because I have interest in it and I feel like I have a connection. I feel like it's something that I'm happy to have studied." After some thought, Ed told me what he would truly like to do, if he did not have to worry about his parents:

I would do social work . . . . My vision is to work on building better relations between races in California. There are already programs like that, but there's room for so much more. Those kinds of jobs, you're not going to associate with being financially secure. I'm putting those wishful things aside and thinking more about trying to do something that's going to fulfill the most of my and my family's needs.

The closed social networks may feel constraining to many children of immigrants, who want to please their parents as well as achieve a sense of personal accomplishment. Their struggle to redefine success, downplay the significance of happiness, repay parental obligations, and construct upwardly mobile career paths illustrates the daily negotiations that children of immigrants must undergo in straddling multiple expectations.

CHAPTER SEVEN

Consumption, Democracy, and the Good Immigrant

> July 4th . . .
> Because my country has sold its soul to corporate power
> Because consumerism has become our national religion
> Because we've forgotten the true meaning of freedom
> And because patriotism now means agreeing with the president
> I pledge to do my duty . . .
> And take my country back.
>
> —Adbusters Media Foundation[1]

The familiar refrain "We are a nation of immigrants" obscures the underlying reality of social citizenship, which makes a clear demarcation between those immigrants who deserve to be members of this society and those who do not. For many immigrants and their children, there is a constant accounting of their worth to determine whether or not they belong—regardless of their actual immigration status. An immigrant's worth is measured primarily in economic terms: taxes paid, cost of social services used, amount of labor input, et cetera.[2] Public opinion polls repeatedly cite immigrants' perceived negative impact on the national economy as the biggest problem. Concerns about immigrants' alleged overuse of social services (including health care, welfare, and education) also reveal a questioning of their worth.[3] In this political environment, immigrants are made to prove their worthiness or patriotism through their economic contribution to and acumen within the market economy. An immigrant's worth is largely measured by imposing an economic value. Those activities or behaviors that are not easily measured are presumed to have no value. Aihwa Ong writes,

Economistic methods and calculations infiltrate areas of social life not primarily economic, regulating behavior to maximize activities that are profitable and marginalize those that are not. Especially since the 1970s, the norms of good citizenship in advanced liberal democracies have shifted from an emphasis on duties and obligations to the nation to a stress on becoming autonomous, responsible choice-making subjects who can serve the nation best by becoming "entrepreneurs of the self."[4]

Thus, good citizenship is increasingly defined in economic terms. In this regard, immigrant entrepreneurs serve an important purpose in demonstrating a model citizenship for ethnic minorities. The political scientist Adolf Reed expresses a similar concern in his assessment of the push for "self-help" among Black Americans. He views this initiative as an effort to replace the standard expectation of democratic citizenship.[5] He writes, "Self-help ideology is a form of privatization and therefore implies cessation of the principle that government is responsible for improving the lives of the citizenry and advancing egalitarian interests . . . "[6] This shift in the norms of good citizenship in American democracy has increasingly emphasized success in strictly economic terms and placed the burden of proving oneself worthy or successful (à la conspicuous consumption) on the individual alone.

This leaves many immigrants in a quandary, given that their mere presence is perceived as a burden upon the nation (and therefore the immigrant must then compensate the true citizens). It is a never-ending cycle in which immigrants feel compelled to justify their presence as legitimate through narrowly prescribed means—consumption—that in the end only works to differentiate them as foreign and unworthy. One of the privileges of full social citizenship is unquestioned acceptance, thereby negating the need to prove one's patriotism and worth. While white Americans do consume, they do not necessarily consume for the same reasons as Asian Americans.[7] In this way, race and class (and I would argue gender) coincide with national ideology to create differential relationships with the state.[8] In fact, the history of citizenship has been one of repeated efforts to limit the rights of citizenship to certain groups—mainly men, whites, and property owners.[9] Those who fall outside of these privileged categories are made to justify their presence.

It is telling that even the children of immigrant entrepreneurs—the supposed epitomes of self-help and good citizenry—must justify their existence. Race, regardless of one's economic performance (via business ownership), remains significant for Asian Americans. No amount of conspicuous consumption can erase one's race. In fact, the actual act of consumption works to highlight the differences that mark Asian Americans as exotic and foreign. In Chapter Three, Sky, who grew up in a homogeneous white community, described the fateful day when she was momentarily stunned by her own reflection in a hallway mirror surrounded by her white friends. Her difference was accentuated by the surroundings. She had grown up thinking she was white—meaning she thought she belonged like everyone else around her. She then set out to acknowledge her Korean identity. However, this was a daunting challenge. As Sky eloquently asked, "How does one force himself/herself to be Korean when they are already Korean?" Those who have the privileges of whiteness rarely ask themselves this question because they are simply *American*.

Sky, on the other hand, feels the burden to justify her racial "difference." Her difficulties with identity formation are understandable, given that Sky and her family have come to epitomize "self-discipline, consumer power, and human entrepreneurial capital" (i.e., "Americanness").[10] It is no surprise that she had thought of herself as "white." In effect, racial categories are political and economic designations of one's place within an unequal social hierarchy. As a young girl, Sky was able to "get by" as American/white until the day she was made to confront her racial marginality. This confrontation left her with limited options. To keep pretending that she was white was not possible—her racial difference could no longer be psychically denied. She was left with the conundrum of how to separate "American" from "whiteness" in order to allow for her presence. She must exert her difference in a way that does not disturb the dominant ideology of American democracy of equality. Conveniently, conspicuous consumption becomes a strategic venue to demonstrate racial difference in a palatable and patriotic way. In accordance with the norms of good citizenship, consumption becomes a patriotic duty for immigrants who want to establish their existence as an economic benefit. One's future career decisions go beyond the individual. According to Sky, like most of her immigrant entrepreneurial peers, her familial role is "to be *very* successful" (her emphasis). This is who she is.

Consequently, there is a conflation of the economic system of capitalism with the political system of democracy, with patriotism measured by economic "benefit." Historically, this conflation became evident immediately following the Great Depression with the institutionalization of the "consuming public" within the National Industrial Recovery Act, a keystone program of the first New Deal initiative.[11] Again, during the Cold War era, there was a concerted effort to define the "American way of life" through mass consumption. Lizabeth Cohen writes: "As the United States justified its superiority over the Soviet Union both at home and abroad, the mass consumption economy offered an arsenal of weapons to defend the reputation of capitalist democracy against the evils of communism."[12] Ironically, an "American capitalist democracy" was promoted as "economic egalitarianism" in response to the Soviet's communist ideal of a classless society.[13] Mass consumption, then, was presented as a form of equal opportunity and the solution to social inequality.

This construction of "rights" as belonging to "consumers" highlights the importance of consumption in defining social citizenship within advanced liberal democracies. Conspicuous consumption is an act of consumptive citizenship. In marketing discourse, Arlene Dávila points out that "'consumers' must prove their value and advertising worthiness through behavior, attitudes, and consumption."[14] Dávila extends this argument and raises the concern that this discourse promotes a "politics of worthiness" that views only those people who can prove their marketability and social worth as entitled to visibility, rights, or services from society.[15] I would extend her concern even further by arguing that the promise of entitlement within this politics of worthiness is an empty one. As Horkheimer and Adorno have stated, the mass consumption industry "perpetually cheats its consumers of what it perpetually promises." I would argue that even when consumers "prove" their marketability and social worth, this does not necessarily entitle them to full citizenship rights. Consumptive citizenship remains illusory for many ethnic minorities, women, and immigrants.

Small Family Businesses: The Do-It-Yourself Solution

It is no coincidence that both Republicans and Democrats tout entrepreneurialism or self-employment as the answer to joblessness and poverty during a time of severe welfare cutbacks. It is a seemingly simple solution—one that requires little effort on behalf of the state. Instead, the Protestant Ethic of virtue associated with individuals "pulling oneself up by the bootstraps" within a merit-based democracy is invoked.[16] During a visit to Chicago, then First Lady Hillary Clinton visited the Women's Self-Employment Project (WSEP)—an entrepreneurial micro-lending organization.[17] The project provides small loans to low-income women who want to open their own businesses but cannot secure bank loans. Clinton commented that support for such projects was essential as the country was implementing welfare reform.[18] Earlier the same year, President Clinton awarded WSEP the Presidential Award for Excellence in Microenterprise Development for "poverty alleviation."[19] Presented as a reform measure to "motivate" people to work, Clinton signed the Personal Responsibility and Work Opportunity Act of 1996, replacing Assistance for Families with Dependent Children (AFDC) entitlements with Temporary Assistance for Needy Families (TANF). TANF makes substantial changes in work requirements for welfare recipients and no longer guarantees access to food stamps and childcare, even for those with young children.[20] This legislative measure is perhaps the most difficult for young and elderly immigrants, whom it bars from nearly every federally funded needs-based welfare program. In the welfare reform bill that passed on August 22, 1996, restrictions on public benefits for *immigrants* accounted for almost half of the total federal savings.[21] A report by the Urban Institute stated that "[e]ven if some of these programs are consolidated into block grants, the reconstituted programs would, presumably, exclude immigrants because they would still be needs based."[22] That is to say, even if these public programs were repackaged through a different funding source, immigrants would still be excluded as undeserving.

Like the national volunteerism campaign and the push to eliminate affirmative action, this welfare legislation is in line with a "do-it-yourself" ideology. In the current age of government devolution, the responsibility for solving social problems like poverty has shifted almost entirely from the federal level to the individual. Perhaps the most egregious element of this do-it-yourself policy is that it allows those who benefit from the poor and their cheap labor to escape unscathed. Such policies exacerbate an already contentious debate about "good" versus "bad" immigrants. They increase the pressure on poor families to fend for themselves while turning a blind eye to the structural realities of today's economy, in which downsizing, transnational labor migration, and expansion of minimum-wage service sector jobs have shifted the social contract from stability to flexibility.[23] Seemingly benign notions like the American Dream, family values, "good" immigrant, and model minority are all similar in their romanticization of the kind of nation we would like to see—but unfortunately the myths fall short of reality. Within this mythology, Asian immigrant entrepreneurs find themselves in a paradox in which they are both scapegoated as burdensome immigrants and placed on a pedestal of positive morality. It is a catch-22 situation in which people scramble over each other in order to be counted as "good" citizens, as defined by the new social welfare state.

The Melancholic Condition of Consumption

In *The Melancholy of Race*, Anne Cheng eloquently characterizes the position of Asian Americans as "suspended." She writes that this suspension takes place within a racial culture that neither fully accepts nor rejects their presence. Cheng describes this experience as "melancholic," in that there is a sense of absence of place while others experience a privilege of belonging. This sense of loss creates a "hole" or gap that needs constant filling—at which point, consumption is encouraged as the primary strategy to fill this emptiness.

Indeed there is an interdependence. Racialization in America operates through the institutional construction of a dominant white national ideal, which is sustained by the exclusion-yet-retention of racialized others.[24] In other words, racialized others are required for the creation and maintenance of the dominant whiteness. Cheng writes, "Racist institutions in fact often do not want to fully expel the racial other; instead, they wish to maintain that other within existing structures. . . . [T]hey need the very thing they hate or fear."[25] In the case of children of Asian immigrant entrepreneurs, they, as racialized others, are needed to continue to straddle the thin line between patriotism and betrayal. Their consumptive efforts communicate a precarious situation: they evidence a constant need for approval, having grown up in a social environment that both needs them and fears them. And, as this study has illustrated, there are costs—for both the Asian American community and the larger U.S. society—to bearing this burden.

Types of Business

American diner
Automobile parts store
Automobile repair shop
Barbershop
Beauty supply store
Car wash
Chinese restaurant
Coin laundromat
Computer repair shop
Computer software store
Construction company
Copy machine repair
Donut shop
Dry cleaners
Fast food chain restaurant
Fortune cookie factory
Grocery store
Hardware store
Herb store

House painting business
Import-export shop
Jewelry store
Karaoke bar
Korean video store
Liquor store
Mail-order business (selling health
    and beauty products)
Martial arts studio
Printing shop
Property management company
Sandwich shop
Sewing machine store
Shoe store
Smoke shop
Souvenir store
Swap-meet business/management
Water filter business

Regional Distribution of Entrepreneurial Respondents

Midwest

    IL 26
    OH 3
    CO 3
    MI 2
    MO 2
    KS 2
    WI 1

West

    CA 24
    HI 1

Northeast

    NY 2
    NJ 1
    NH 1

South

    TX 2
    GA 1

Total 71

Notes

1. Lee 2000.
2. Hernandez and Glenn 2003:419.
3. See Kibria 2002; Portes and Rumbaut 2001; Rumbaut and Portes 2001; Bankston and Zhou 1998; Suarez-Orozco and Suarez-Orozco 2001.
4. However, there are some notable exceptions within the social sciences, including Abelmann and Lie 1995; Glenn 1986; Hondagneu-Sotelo 2001; Light and Bonacich 1988; Siu 1987; Maira 2002; Espiritu 2003.
5. See Abelmann and Lie 1995:147.
6. This is not to imply that consumption is unique to Asian Americans, of course, or that conspicuous consumption would be a useful tool in analyzing the political economic position of only Asian Americans. In fact, I would argue that a critical analysis of consumption is a fruitful intellectual exercise towards a deeper understanding of various racial/ethnic, class, and gender/sexuality based communities.
7. bell hooks (2000) cites Stuart and Elizabeth Ewen (1982) in making this point.
8. See Garcia Canclini 2001; O'Dougherty 2002.
9. See Lamphere 1992.
10. See Ablemann and Lie 1995; Osajima 1988.
11. See Yoon 1997.
12. Fraser and Gordon 1998:114.

13. Fraser and Gordon 1998:114.

14. Fraser and Gordon 1998:116.

15. However, it is technically incorrect to address the experiences of Asian Americans raised in the United States as immigrant adaptation or assimilation, given that as Americans, Asian Americans have presumably already "adapted." In this respect, children of immigrants are frequently misidentified as immigrants. This misclassification has real implications for the second generation (as well as generations thereafter) in that perceptions of "foreignness" and marginalization through Orientalism continue to persist.

16. Hernandez and Glenn (2003:419) critique this traditional "status-attainment framework" for focusing on individual mobility and assuming the "necessity of immigrants fitting into a preexisting hierarchy," as opposed to challenging the unequal power structure.

17. See Saito 2001; Goode and Schneider 1994.

18. Goode and Schneider 1994:15–16.

19. Saito 2001:336.

20. Perea 1997.

21. Delgado 1997.

22. See Dávila 2001:11. Also, feminist scholars Kathleen Canning and Sonya O. Rose (2001:427) describe citizenship as "[o]ne of the most porous concepts in contemporary academic parlance [that] can be understood as a political status assigned to individuals by states, as a relation of belonging to specific communities, or as a set of social practices that defines the relationships between peoples and states and among peoples within communities."

23. See also Lowe 1996; and A. Ong 1999.

24. See Glenn 2002; Sarvasy 1997; and Yuval-Davis 1997.

25. Leland Saito (2001:335) invokes this idea in his study of Japanese Americans and new Chinese immigrants in Monterey Park, California. He writes, " . . . they tried to adapt in ways that would minimize anti-Japanese tendencies by conforming to the 'good immigrant' ideal."

26. Saito 2001.

27. Delgado 1997.

28. This is certainly apparent in recent immigration policies, which have increasingly favored "professional" or "investor" immigrants from Asian countries (J. Park 2003; Li and E. Park 2003).

29. In the September 29, 2002, issue of the *New York Times Magazine*, the film critic A. O. Scott writes, "About a year ago, in a burst of patriotism, my wife and I went out and bought a car. Well, yes, it was a Swedish car, but at the time this perfectly ordinary act of conspicuous consumption felt like—and more to

the point, was being widely promoted as—an act of civic duty."

30. Reacting to the exploitation of the U.S. flag as a corporate logo in an effort to sell itself as "more patriotic than thou," *New York Times* commentator Frank Rich (July 6, 2003) writes, "Such flag-waving for personal and corporate profit has gotten so out of hand that last month, when the House of Representatives passed a constitutional amendment banning flag desecration for the umpteenth time, I for once found myself rooting for the Senate to follow suit. It would be fun to watch TV executives hauled on to Court TV. If NBC's post-9 / 11 decision to slap the flag on screen in the shape of its trademarked peacock wasn't flag desecration, what is?"

31. Tuan 1998.

32. Portes (1997:814) cites Robert Merton (1987:10–11) in making this point. Also, Min Zhou (1997:64) adds, "Until the recent past, scholarly attention has focused on adult immigrants to the neglect of child immigrants and immigrant offspring, creating a profound gap between the strategic importance of these children and the knowledge about their conditions."

33. Rosenblatt 1999:3.

34. Rosenblatt 1999:2.

35. See Luttwak 1999.

36. Juliet Schor (1999:38) states that "personal prejudice and a political preference for conclusions that celebrate a free consumer market have led economists to an uncritical and simplistic approach to consumer behavior: virtually without question, whatever consumers do is in their own best interest."

37. Schor 1999:40.

38. Veblen 1899:70.

39. Schor (1999:41) explains that " . . . consumption yields well-being or satisfaction not on the basis of its absolute level but always in relation to the level of consumption others have achieved."

40. See Halle 1993.

41. See Bourdieu 2000; Holt 2000; Ewen and Ewen 1982.

42. She writes, "The new consumerism is more anonymous and is less socially benign than the old regime of keeping up with the Joneses. . . . People are now more likely to compare themselves with, or aspire to the lifestyles of, those far above them in the economic hierarchy" (1999:43).

43. Lowe 1996:162. She (1996:4) also states that "in the last century and a half, the American citizen has been defined over against the Asian immigrant, legally, economically, and culturally. These definitions have cast Asian immigrants both as persons and populations to be integrated into the national political sphere and as the contradictory, confusing, unintelligible elements to be mar-

ginalized and returned to their alien origins."

44. In *Crafting Selves*, Dorinne K. Kondo (1990) notes that identity is constantly in motion and, not unexpectedly, the ritual of consuming also follows suit.

45. In Ann DuCille's (2000) work on multicultural Barbie dolls, she found that difference was permitted only in "discursively familiar" ways. The consumer society requires that a Barbie, regardless of her color, retain the body and the class status of the normative (white) Barbie.

46. Kotlowitz 2000.

47. hooks 2000:356.

48. Horkheimer and Adorno 1972.

49. See Gordon 1997.

50. Ehrenreich 1989; Newman 1988; L. Rubin 1994.

51. See Rubin 1994.

52. See also L. Park 2002; Ablemann and Lie 1995.

53. Abelmann and Lie 1995:ix.

54. However, Korean Americans do have the highest rate of self-employment in the United States, at 24.3 percent, and Chinese Americans are just above the national average, at 10.8 percent (Yoon 1997).

55. Kim 2000.

56. Kim 2000:10.

57. Kim 2000:16.

58. Dávila 2001:13, 202.

59. Espiritu 2003:48.

60. Espiritu makes this point specifically about Filipino migration, but I would extend the analogy to other Asian Americans as well. Traditional immigration narratives obscure the reality of initial East-West relationships, which were based upon international trade forced upon Asia in the name of Western imperialism. For instance, Evelyn Nakano Glenn (1986:23) notes that the United States had a powerful presence in Asia given their need for cheap labor during the first wave of migration from Asia between 1850 and the 1930s. She writes: "As an imperial power the United States could exact treaties and agreements that permitted recruitment of labor under advantageous terms. Special liabilities, such as denial of naturalization rights, could be imposed on Asian immigrants, making them more controllable than native whites or Europeans."

61. A. Ong 2003.

62. See A. Ong 1999:180.

63. Yoon 1997.
64. Yoon 1997:14.
65. Abelmann and Lie 1995:136.
66. Borjas 1990; Portes 1994.
67. See Light and Bonacich 1988; Portes and Zhou 1993.
68. Abelmann and Lie 1995:147.
69. Yoon 1997:6.
70. Glaser and Strauss 1967.
71. All names of interviewees, their families, and businesses are pseudonyms.
72. Strauss 1987.
73. According to the 1990 Census, 24.3 percent of Koreans living in the United States own their own business, making them the highest ranked. Chinese Americans hover just above the national average (10.2 percent), at 10.8 percent.
74. The term "1.5 generation" implies that the individual was born in the sending country but grew up in the host country. Although there are no strict rules, those who arrive as teenagers are generally considered first generation.

CHAPTER TWO

1. Cha 1982:81.
2. Daniels 1997.
3. Immigration to the United States is broadly understood as consisting of four major waves: (1) Northwest Europeans in the mid-nineteenth century; (2) Southern and Eastern Europeans at the end of the nineteenth century and beginning of the twentieth; (3) African Americans, Mexicans, and Puerto Ricans to the North from the South precipitated by two World Wars; and (4) Latin Americans and Asians from 1965 to the present (Muller and Espenshade 1985).
4. This is not to imply that lawmakers at the time actually intended to alter the racial composition of immigrants. In fact, they did not (Jiobu 1996).
5. Portes and Rumbaut 2001:21.
6. 1990 U.S. Census figures from Zhou 1997.
7. See Hing 1993:41–42.
8. S. Chan 1990:61–62.
9. S. Chan 1990:66.
10. Louie 2004:xvii.
11. A. Ong 1987:4–5.

12. Nancy Landale (1997) pointed out that neither research nor theory on immigration systematically addressed the complexity of second-generation experiences, despite their centrality in understanding the process of adaptation.

13. These works include Portes and Zhou 1993; Gans 1992; Rumbaut 1994; Waters 1999; Zhou 1997; Wolf 1997; Zhou and Bankston 1998; Hernandez and Charney 1998; Tuan 1998; Song 1999; Portes and Rumbaut 2001; Suarez-Orozco and Suarez-Orozco 2001; Min 2002; Maira 2002; Kibria 2002; Danico 2004; Louie 2004.

14. Handlin 1951.

15. Tilly 1990.

16. Fernandez-Kelly and Schauffler 1994; Portes 1994; Light and Bonacich 1988. For instance, in their study of immigrant children from Haiti, Vietnam, Cuba, Nicaragua, and Mexico, Fernandez-Kelly and Schauffler found that immigration was a phenomenon of labor mobility. In line with the social network focus of the new economic sociology, the authors explained this phenomenon as a result of interpersonal networks bridging points of origin and points of destination.

17. Sassen 1995.

18. Portes 1994:5.

19. Rumbaut 1994:783.

20. Hernandez and Glenn 2003:419.

21. Portes 1997.

22. Espiritu 2003:208.

23. Espiritu 2003:4.

24. Espiritu 2003:47.

25. Henry Yu (2001:102) critiques narratives that interpret experiences and conflicts within immigrant communities as an indication of "assimilation" as ahistorical. He states that this recurring use of the term "assimilation," regardless of historical period, exoticizes the Asian American experience by constructing a "foreign" culture as the explanation for something that may exist in non-immigrant families.

26. Schor and Holt 2000:xv.

27. This was made clear in the 2004 presidential election, in which media consultants for George W. Bush's re-election campaign conducted a detailed study of Americans' consumer behavior to guide their successful political advertising strategy (Seelve 2004).

28. Of course, this is not the case for every immigrant, including Chinese

immigrants emigrating from Southeast Asian countries such as Vietnam and Singapore.

29. In the first wave, there were approximately 7,200 Koreans who came to work in the sugar plantations of Hawaii (Kibria 2002:23).

30. See Kibria 2002:24.

31. Louie 2004:xxii.

32. Louie 2004:xxii; Kwong 1997.

33. Kibria 2002:24.

34. The economic, political, and military influence of the United States in South Korea has been intense since the end of World War II (Yoon 1997:61).

35. Min 1995.

36. S. Chan (1990:52) also notes that during the Japanese occupation of Korea, Koreans were forbidden from participating in the import-export trade.

37. S. Chan 1990:52.

38. Yoon 1997:55.

39. Yoon 1997:92.

40. Kibria (2002:19) also came to the same conclusion in her study: "I began the study with the idea that the clear-cut differences in population concentration—of Asians, Chinese, and Koreans—between the two areas would make a difference to patterns of adaptation and identity. These effects ultimately turned out to be far less pronounced than I had expected."

41. As predicted by Yoon, Kwong, and others.

42. The 1990 Census reports the median family income for Chinese Americans at $41,316, and $33,909 for Korean Americans. Korean American families also have a higher percentage of poverty (Kibria 2002:24).

43. U.S. Small Business Administration (hereafter abbreviated as SBA) 2001.

44. These figures are before business expenses, costs, and taxes.

45. SBA 2001:12.

46. SBA 2001:22.

47. SBA 2001:22. Among the highest survival rates by industry for minority-owned businesses, that of Black-owned businesses in legal services was 79.1 percent and that of Latino (Hispanic)-owned businesses in health services was 65.6 percent.

48. Yoon 1997:141. *Kyes* are usually composed of ten to twenty people, who contribute an equal amount of money to a fund that is lent to each of them in rotating order. All kye members, including the borrower, continue to make monthly payments until everyone benefits from the fund (Yoon 1997:144). As early as 1962, Clifford Geertz cited the existence of such associations around the world, including Japan, China, Southeast Asia, India, West Africa, and the

Caribbean (Geertz in Granovetter 1995b).

49. Light et al. 1993.

50. U.S. Department of Commerce 1997.

51. See Tuan 1998:77.

52. Yoon 1997:48.

53. Kibria 2002:12. Author's emphasis.

CHAPTER THREE

1. See Coontz 1992.

2. See Taylor 1989.

3. Hochschild (2003:37–39) describes the growing "commodity frontier" of families as an important market niche.

4. Pyke 2000.

5. Pyke 2000:240.

6. Nippert-Eng 1996.

7. This figure is in comparison to 41 percent for the seventeen children in the non-entrepreneurial comparison sample of Korean and Chinese American children of immigrants interviewed in this study.

8. Gillis 1996:4.

9. Hall 1983.

10. Gillis 1996:4. See also Hareven 1982.

11. Hochschild (2003:38) writes, "Between 1989 and 1996 . . . middle-class married couples increased their annual work hours outside the home from 3,550 to 3,685, or more than three extra forty-hour weeks of work a year."

12. Ong and Hee 1994.

13. Hochschild 1997:13–14.

14. Rohner and Pettingill 1985.

15. Greeley 1987.

16. Song (1999:61) identifies three levels of labor involvement by immigrant children in small family businesses: (1) *integral*—intense caring work and a significant role within the family business; (2) *supplemental*—some caring work and some role within the family business; and (3) *minor*—no caring work and no regular work at the business.

17. Similar to the ways that children deal with premature adulthood and prolonged childhood within immigrant entrepreneurial homes, parents also negotiate status/role inconsistencies. In their dependence upon their children, the parents also undergo a form of "childification." Song (1999) also observed this dynamic.

18. A popular sit-com of the 1980s and early 1990s, in which friends congregate regularly at a neighborhood bar.

19. A number of other respondents (four) also described similar frustrations with the difference in their parents' behavior around customers/others and around their children. These frustrations arose during the children's high school years as they watched their parent's interactions at the store.

20. Beyond physical maturation (i.e., puberty), I am alluding to a more psychological and sociological understanding of ego development, wherein maturity is gained through successful attainment of an integrated, realistic self-concept that is the basis for further identity development. See Susan Harter 1990:352–87.

21. However, it is noteworthy that whether or not a business is successful generally has little bearing on how the child views the parent. A failed business does not necessarily result in a failed parent. More than half of my sample had experienced more than one business failure in their lifetime, and yet in their entrepreneurial narratives, the parent continued to hold the role of the hero. The fact that persistent business failure does not imply parental failure is a strong testament to the importance of successful boundary work.

22. See Granovetter 1995a; Nee and Nee 1972; Zhou 1992.

23. A popular television drama in the 1970s and early 1980s about a rural family during the Depression.

24. See Coontz 1992.

25. Light and Bonacich 1988:356.

26. Light and Bonacich 1988:365.

27. Light and Bonacich 1988:7.

28. Light and Bonacich 1988:435.

29. Light and Bonacich 1988:355.

CHAPTER FOUR

1. As Song (1999:16) writes, " . . . experiences of racism, discrimination, and social marginalization could intensify feelings of family solidarity."

2. Sanders and Nee 1996:235.

3. Zelizer 1985.

4. Platt 1969.

5. Brooks-Gunn and Reiter 1990.

6. Song 1999:15.

7. These roles also required that the children perform added responsibilities as problem solvers and translators for their parents. See L. Park 2001; L. Park 2002.

8. In making this argument, I make a general differentiation between child and adult, but with the understanding that there are significant nuances and developmental levels within each category (e.g., adolescence).

9. K. Park 1997:3.

10. Miri Song (1999:57), in her study of immigrant Chinese young adults who work with their parents in Chinese take-aways in England, defines caring work as "assisting, accompanying, and translating for parents."

11. However, there were two respondents who worked for their family businesses as adults, who received compensation comparable to other employees for their labor.

12. Abelmann and Lie 1995; Light and Bonacich 1988.

13. Thomas 1967.

14. See Nee and Nee 1972:168.

15. Greenberger and Steinberg 1986.

16. Greenberger and Steinberg 1986.

17. Sung 1987:183.

18. Collins 1991; King 1990.

19. Burton et al. 1996.

20. *New York Times* Aug. 15, 1991.

CHAPTER FIVE

1. Bredahl 1989:148.

2. There are also revisionist and spaghetti Western narratives. See *http://history.acusd.edu/gen/filmnotes/western-narrative.html.*

3. Maynard 1974:vi.

4. Those few who deem their parents' business a failure also deem their parenting a failure as well. In which case, these respondents do not employ these themes in their narrative. This is discussed further in Chapter Six.

5. Decker 1997.

6. This is not to imply that more overt confrontation or racist behavior does not take place. In separate interviews with parents, several mothers conceded that they kept some of the most hostile interactions with customers to themselves, not telling their children because they did not want to worry or upset them.

7. That is, dutiful respect for parents.

8. See Pellow and Park 2002; Espiritu 2003.

9. Lowe (1996:5) points out that " . . . [T]he project of imagining the nation as homogeneous requires the orientalist construction of cultures and geographies from which Asian immigrants come as fundamentally 'foreign' origins and

antipathetic to the modern American society that 'discovers,' 'welcomes,' and 'domesticates' them."

10. Dávila (2001:219) adds: "All of these marginal others need to be repeatedly reminded that they too are part of the United States and that their contributions 'enrich' or 'empower' this country because, regardless of their history or citizenship status, they remain 'foreigners' or virtual foreigners vis-à-vis the 'general public' by the nature of their race, ethnicity, and culture, and the values and behaviors that are ascribed to them by such differences."

11. B. Rubin 1996; Sassen 1988; Yoon 1997.

12. In her study of waitresses at a roadside diner, Paules (1993:69–170) describes female occupations in this way: "Each detail of the work process is regulated by the company; job tasks center on the performance of traditional female duties: serving, waiting, smiling, flattering; and emphasize putatively female qualities: patience, sociability, submissiveness; and there are no meaningful opportunities to advance."

13. Bonacich 1973.

14. Siu 1987.

15. Hing 1993.

16. Siu 1987:47.

17. Siu 1987:45.

18. Nee and Nee 1972.

19. Siu 1987:51.

20. Siu 1987:53.

21. For example, as late as 1973, employee handbooks stated that women were better suited for typing because they had shorter thumbs (*Chicago Reader*, 3 / 27 / 98, p. 42).

22. Siu 1987.

23. Siu 1987:54.

24. J. Chan 1998:94.

25. J. Chan 1998:100.

26. J. Chan 1998:100.

27. Siu 1987:9.

28. Eng 2001:17.

29. This is evidenced in the recent HBO film *Better Luck Tomorrow*, which depicts the detrimental effects of stereotypes on Asian American young men living in Orange County, California.

30. It should be noted that most men, regardless of race, fall far short of this hetero-masculine ideal and that not everyone wants to strive towards such a goal.

31. Pyke and Johnson 2003.

32. K. Park 1997.

33. Hollingshead 1949.

34. Elder et al. 1993:7.

35. Reskin and Padavic 1994:4.

36. L. Rubin 1994.

37. Larson and Richards 1994.

38. Section title adapted from Vijay Prashad's (2001) book, *Everybody Was Kung Fu Fighting.*

39. Prashad 2001:128–29.

CHAPTER SIX

1. These self-designated class categories have little to do with their family's actual household income levels. Most of the respondents did not have a clear idea of how much their family made each year. Almost everyone simply made an educated guess of "middle class."

2. See Nippert-Eng 1996.

3. Gans 1992. Not to mention that many of these respondents now come from cosmopolitan cities within advanced societies, for whom the notion of the "old country" is less relevant.

4. Coleman 1988:104–5.

5. Admittedly, the lack of respondents who were not college bound is a limitation of this study.

CHAPTER SEVEN

1. Adbusters Media Foundation advertisement, *New York Times* July 3, 2003, A9.

2. See Borjas 1990.

3. California's Proposition 187, for instance, denied public K–12 and postsecondary education to undocumented immigrant school children and cut off publicly funded non-emergency medical care, welfare benefits, and other social services to undocumented immigrants. The measure passed, but it was never enacted, due to successful lawsuits that found the measure unconstitutional. Similar kinds of legislative measures that promote this image of immigrant welfare dependency continue regardless of the fact that immigrants' overall use of welfare is roughly the same as natives' (Fix and Passel 1999).

4. A. Ong 2003:9.

5. Reed 2000.

6. Reed 2000:59.

7. Ong (2003:11) states: "Historically, the intertwining of race and economic performance has shaped the ways in which different immigrant groups have attained status and dignity, within national ideology that projects worthy citizens as inherently white."

8. Glenn (2002:55) writes: "For nonwhite people and women, citizenship has always been a malleable structure, molded by the efforts of dominant groups seeking to enforce their own definitions of citizenship and its boundaries, and by the efforts of subordinated groups to contest these definitions and boundaries. Thus the meaning of citizenship has evolved over time, has varied by place, and has differed for different people."

9. Delgado 1997; Hall and Held 1990:175; Glenn 2002:20.

10. A. Ong 2003.

11. See Cohen 2003:19. As part of this program, a consumer advisory board was established, which included representatives of the "consuming public" alongside business and labor leaders. One member of this board was the prominent Columbia University sociologist Robert S. Lynd, who argued that the viability of American democracy depended upon the quality of living that its citizens could achieve.

12. Cohen 2003:124.

13. Cohen 2003:125.

14. Dávila 2001:237.

15. Dávila 2001:237.

16. See Richard Weiss 1969; Decker 1997.

17. Micro-enterprises are very small businesses, with up to five employees.

18. Breslin and Sweeney 1997.

19. WSEP press package.

20. Moses 1997.

21. MaCurdy and O'Brien-Strain 1998.

22. Fix and Zimmerman 1997:250.

23. L. Rubin 1994.

24. Cheng 2000:10.

25. Cheng 2000:12.

References

Abelmann, Nancy, and John Lie. 1995. *Blue Dreams: Korean Americans and the Los Angeles Riots.* Cambridge, Mass.: Harvard University Press.

Alger, Horatio, Jr. 1945. *Struggling Upward and Other Works.* Edited by Russel Crouse. New York: Crown Publishers.

Bankston, Carl, and Min Zhou. 1998. Growing Up American: *How Vietnamese Children Adapt to Life in the United States.* New York: Russell Sage Foundation.

Bonacich, Edna. 1973. A Theory of Middleman Minorities. *American Sociological Review* 38: 583–94.

Borjas, George J. 1990. *Friends or Strangers: The Impact of Immigrants on the U.S. Economy.* New York: Basic Books, Inc.

Bourdieu, Pierre. 2000. The Aesthetic Sense as the Sense of Distinction (1979; translated 1984). In *Consumer Society Reader,* edited by Juliet Schor and Douglas B. Holt, 205–11. New York: The New Press.

Bredahl, Carl, Jr. 1989. *New Ground: Western American Narrative and the Literary Canon.* Chapel Hill: University of North Carolina Press.

Breslin, Meg M., and Annie Sweeney. 1997. First Lady's Wish Is to Help Women, Children Overcome. *Chicago Tribune,* Feb. 19.

Brooks-Gunn, Jeanne, and Edward O. Reiter. 1990. The Role of Pubertal Processes. In *At the Threshold: The Developing Adolescent,* edited by S. Shirley Feldman and Glen R. Elliott, 16–53. Cambridge, MA: Harvard University Press.

Burton, Linda M., Dawn Obeidallah, and Kevin Allison. 1996. Ethnographic

Insights on Social Context and Adolescent Development Among Inner-City African-American Teens. In *Essays on Ethnography and Human Development*, edited by Richard Jessor, A. Colby, and Richard A. Shweder, 397–418. Chicago: University of Chicago Press.

Canning, Kathleen, and Sonya O. Rose. 2001. Gender, Citizenship, and Subjectivity: Some Historical and Theoretical Considerations. *Gender and Society* 13(3): 427–43.

Cha, Theresa Hak Kyung. 1982. *Dictee*. New York: Tanam Press.

Chan, Jachinson. 1998. Contemporary Asian American Men's Issues. In *Teaching Asian America: Diversity and the Problem of Community*, edited by Lane Ryo Hirabayashi, 93–102. Lanham, MD: Rowman & Littlefield.

Chan, Sucheng. 1990. European and Asian Immigration into the United States in Comparative Perspective, 1820s to 1920s. In *Immigration Reconsidered: History, Sociology, and Politics*, edited by Virginia Yans-McLanghlin, 37–75. New York: Oxford University Press.

Cheng, Anne Anlin. 2000. *The Melancholy of Race*. Oxford and New York: Oxford University Press.

Cohen, Lizabeth. 2003. *A Consumers' Republic*. New York: Knopf.

Coleman, James. 1988. Social Capital in the Creation of Human Capital. *American Journal of Sociology* 94: 95–120.

Collins, Patricia H. 1991. *Black Feminist Thought*. New York: Routledge.

Coontz, Stephanie. 1992. *The Way We Never Were: American Families and the Nostalgia Trap*. New York: Basic Books.

Danico, Mary Yu. 2004. *The 1.5 Generation: Becoming Korean American in Hawaii*. Honolulu: University of Hawaii Press.

Daniels, Roger. 1997. No Lamps Were Lit for Them: Angel Island and the Historiography of Asian American Immigration. *Journal of American Ethnic History* 17(1): 3–18.

Dávila, Arlene. 2001. *Latinos, Inc.: The Marketing and Making of a People*. Berkeley: University of California Press.

Decker, Jeffrey L. 1997. *Made in America: Self-Styled Success from Horatio Alger to Oprah Winfrey*. Minneapolis: University of Minnesota Press.

Delgado, Richard. 1997. Citizenship. In *Immigrants Out! The New Nativism and the Anti-Immigrant Impulse in the United States*, edited by Juan F. Perea, 318–23. New York: New York University Press.

Du Bois, W. E. B. 1903. *The Souls of Black Folk*. Chicago: A. C. McClurg & Co.

DuCille, Ann. 2000. Toy Theory: Black Barbie and the Deep Play of Difference. In *Consumer Society Reader*, edited by Juliet Schor and Douglas B. Holt, 259–80. New York: The New Press.

Ehrenreich, Barbara. 1989. *Fear of Falling: The Inner Life of the Middle Class.* New York: Pantheon Books.

Elder, Glen H., Jr., John Modell, and Ross D. Parke. 1993. *Children in Time and Place: Developmental and Historical Insights.* Cambridge: Cambridge University Press.

Eng, David. 2001. *Racial Castration: Managing Masculinity in Asian America.* Durham, N.C.: Duke University Press.

Espiritu, Yen Le. 2003. *Homebound: Filipino American Lives Across Countries, Communities, and Countries.* Berkeley: University of California Press.

Ewen, Stuart, and Elizabeth Ewen. 1982. *Channels of Desire: Mass Images and the Shaping of American Consciousness.* New York: McGraw-Hill.

Fanon, Frantz. 1967. *Black Skin, White Masks.* New York: Grove Press.

Fernandez-Kelly, M. Patricia, and Richard Schauffler. 1994. Divided Fates: Immigrant Children in a Restructured U.S. Economy. *International Migration Review* 28: 662–89.

Fix, Michael, and Jeffrey S. Passel. 1999. *Trends in Noncitizens' and Citizens' Use of Public Benefits Following Welfare Reform: 1995–1997.* Washington, DC: The Urban Institute.

Fix, Michael, and Wendy Zimmerman. 1997. Immigrant Families and Public Policy a Deepening Divide. In *Immigration and the Family: Research and Policy on U.S. Immigrants*, edited by A. Booth et al., 237–61. New York: Lawrence Erlbaum.

Fraser, Nancy, and Linda Gordon. 1998. Contract Versus Charity: Why Is There No Social Citizenship in the United States? In *The Citizenship Debates*, edited by Gershon Shafir, 113–27. Minneapolis: University of Minnesota Press.

Fuchs, Victor R. 1991. Are Americans Underinvesting in Their Children? *Society* Sept. / Oct.: 14–22.

Gans, Herbert J. 1992. Second Generation Decline: Scenarios for the Economic and Ethnic Futures of Post-1965 American Immigrants. *Ethnic and Racial Studies* 15: 173–92.

Garcia Canclini, Néstor. 2001. *Consumers and Citizens: Globalization and Multicultural Conflicts.* Minneapolis: University of Minnesota Press.

Geertz, Clifford. 1962. The Rotating Credit Association: A "Middle Rung" in Development. *Economic Development and Cultural Change* 10(3): 243.

Gillis, John. 1996. Making Time for Family: The Invention of Family Time(s) and the Reinvention of Family History. *Journal of Family History* 21(1): 4–22.

Glaser, Barney G., and Anselm L. Strauss. 1967. *The Discovery of Grounded Theory.* Chicago: Aldine Publishing Co.

Glenn, Evelyn Nakano. 1986. *Issei, Nisei, War Bride.* Philadelphia: Temple University Press.

————.2002. *Unequal Freedom: How Race and Gender Shaped American Citizenship and Labor*. Cambridge, MA: Harvard University Press.

Goode, Judith, and Jo Anne Schneider. 1994. *Reshaping Ethnic and Racial Relations in Philadelphia: Immigrants in a Divided City*. Philadelphia: Temple University Press.

Gordon, Avery. 1997. *Ghostly Matters: Haunting and the Sociological Imagination*. Minneapolis: University of Minnesota Press.

Granovetter, Mark. 1995a. *Getting a Job: A Study of Contacts and Careers*. Chicago: University of Chicago Press. Second edition.

————. 1995b. The Economic Sociology of Firms and Entrepreneurs. In *The Economic Sociology of Immigration: Essays on Networks, Ethnicity, and Entrepreneurship*, edited by Alejandro Portes, 128–65. New York: Russell Sage Foundation.

Greeley, Andrew. 1987. Today's Morality Play: The Sitcom. *New York Times*, May 17.

Greenberger, Ellen. 1984. Children, Families, and Work. In *Children, Mental Health, and the Law*, edited by N. Dickon Reppucci et al., 103–24. Beverly Hills, CA: Sage Publications.

————, and Laurence Steinberg. 1986. *When Teenagers Work*. New York: Basic Books.

Hall, Edward T. 1983. *The Dance of Life: The Other Dimensions of Time*. New York: Anchor Books.

Hall, Stuart, and David Held. 1990. Citizens and Citizenship. In *New Times: The Changing Face of Politics in the 1990s*, edited by Stuart Hall and Martin Jacques. New York: Verso.

Halle, David. 1993. *Inside Culture: Art and Class in the American Home*. Chicago: University of Chicago Press.

Handlin, Oscar. 1951. *The Uprooted*. Boston: Little, Brown.

Hareven, Tamara. 1982. *Family Time and Industrial Time*. Cambridge: Cambridge University Press.

Harter, Susan. 1990. Adolescent Self and Identity Development. In *At the Threshold: The Developing Adolescent*, edited by S. Shirley Feldman and Glen R. Elliott, 352–87. Cambridge, MA: Harvard University Press.

Hernandez, David Manuel, and Evelyn Nakano Glenn. 2003. Ethnic Prophecies: A Review Essay. *Contemporary Sociology* 32(4): 418–26.

Hernandez, Donald J., and Evan Charney. 1998. *From Generation to Generation: The Health and Well-Being of Children in Immigrant Families*. Washington, DC: National Academy Press.

Hing, Bill Ong. 1993. *Making and Remaking Asian America Through Immigration Policy, 1850–1990*. Stanford, CA: Stanford University Press.

Hochschild, Arlie Russell. 1997. *The Time Bind*. New York: Metropolitan Books.
———.2003. *The Commercialization of Intimate Life*. Berkeley: University of California Press.

Hollingshead, August de Belmont. 1949. *Elmtown's Youth: The Impact of Social Classes on Adolescents*. New York: J. Wiley.

Holt, Douglas B. 2000. Does Cultural Capital Structure American Consumption? In *Consumer Society Reader*, edited by Juliet Schor and Douglas B. Holt, 212–52. New York: The New Press.

———, and Juliet B. Schor. 2000. Introduction: Do Americans Consume Too Much? In *Consumer Society Reader*, edited by Juliet B. Schor and Douglas B. Holt, vii–xxiii. New York: The New Press.

Hondagneu-Sotelo, Pierette. 2001. *Doméstica: Immigrant Workers Cleaning and Caring in the Shadows of Affluence*. Berkeley: University of California Press.

hooks, bell. 2000. Eating the Other: Desire and Resistance. In *The Consumer Society Reader*, edited by Juliet B. Schor and Douglas B. Holt, 343–59. New York: The New Press.

Horkheimer, Max, and Theodor W. Adorno. 1972. 2000 reprint. *Dialectic of Enlightenment*. Translated by John Cumming. New York: Continuum.

Hughes, C. Everett. 1967. *The Sociological Eye*. Chicago: Aldine-Atherton.

Jiobu, Robert M. 1996. Recent Asian Pacific Immigrants: The Demographic Background. In *Reframing the Immigration Debate*, edited by Bill Ong Hing and Ronald Lee, 35–58. Los Angeles: LEAP Asian Pacific American Public Policy Institute.

Kibria, Nazli. 2002. *Becoming Asian American: Second-Generation Chinese and Korean American Identities*. Baltimore: Johns Hopkins University Press.

Kim, Claire Jean. 2000. *Bitter Fruit: The Politics of Black-Korean Conflict in New York City*. New Haven, CT: Yale University Press.

King, Deborah. 1990. Multiple Jeopardy, Multiple Consciousness: The Context of a Black Feminist Ideology. In *Black Women in America,* edited by Micheline R. Malson et al., 265–97. Chicago: University of Chicago Press.

Kondo, Dorinne K. 1990. *Crafting Selves: Power, Gender, and Discourses of Identity in a Japanese Workplace*. Chicago: University of Chicago Press.

Kotlowitz, Alex. 2000. False Connections. In *The Consumer Society Reader*, edited by Juliet B. Schor and Douglas B. Holt, 253–58. New York: The New Press.

Kwong, Peter. 1997. *Forbidden Workers: Illegal Chinese Immigrants and American Labor*. New York: The New Press.

Lamphere, Louise. 1992. *Structuring Diversity: Ethnographic Perspectives on the New Immigration*. Chicago: University of Chicago Press.

Landale, Nancy S. 1997. Immigration and the Family: An Overview. In

Immigration and the Family: Research and Policy on U.S. Immigrants, edited by A. Booth et al., 281–92. New York: Lawrence Erlbaum.

Larson, Reed, and Maryse H. Richards. 1994. *Divergent Realities: The Emotional Lives of Mothers, Fathers, and Adolescents*. New York: Basic Books.

Lee, T. A. 2000. A Good Son. *A Magazine* Oct. / Nov.: 18–20.

Li, Wei, and Edward J. W. Park. 2003. Asian Americans and Latinos in Silicon Valley: Immigration Policies, Transnational Capital, and Community Transitions. Paper presented at the Annual Meeting of the Association of Asian American Studies, May 10.

Light, Ivan H., and Edna Bonacich. 1988. *Immigrant Entrepreneurs: Koreans in Los Angeles, 1965–1982*. Berkeley: University of California Press.

Light, Ivan H., Parminder Bhachu, and Stavros Karageorgis. 1993. Migration Networks and Immigrant Entrepreneurship. In *Immigration and Entrepreneurship: Culture, Capital, and Ethnic Networks*, edited by Ivan H. Light and Parminder Bhachu, 25–50. New Brunswick, NJ: Transaction Publishers.

Lorde, Audre. 1984. *Sister Outsider: Essays and Speeches*. Trumansburg, NY: Crossing Press.

Louie, Vivian S. 2004. *Compelled to Excel: Immigration, Education, and Opportunity Among Chinese Americans*. Stanford, CA: Stanford University Press.

Lowe, Lisa. 1996. *Immigrant Acts: On Asian American Cultural Politics*. Durham, NC: Duke University Press.

Luttwak, Edward N. 1999. Consuming for Love. In *Consuming Desires*, edited by Roger Rosenblatt, 51–64. Washington, DC: Island Press.

MaCurdy, Thomas, and Margaret O'Brien-Strain. 1998. *Reform Reversed? The Restoration of Welfare Benefits to Immigrants in California*. San Francisco: Public Policy Institute of California.

Maira, Sunaina Marr. 2002. *Desis in the House: Indian American Youth Culture in New York City*. Philadelphia: Temple University Press.

Marshall, T. H. 1964. Citizenship and Social Class. In *Class, Citizenship, and Social Development: Essays by T. H. Marshall*, edited by Seymour Martin Lipset. Chicago: University of Chicago Press.

Maynard, Richard A. 1974. *The American West on Film: Myth and Reality*. Rochelle Park, NJ: Hayden Book Co.

Merton, Robert. 1987. Three Fragments from a Sociologist's Notebook: Establishing the Phenomenon, Specified Ignorance, and Strategic Research Materials. *Annual Review of Sociology* 13: 1–28.

Min, Pyong Gap. 1995. Korean Americans. In *Asian Americans: Contemporary*

Trends and Issues, edited by Pyong Gap Min, 199–231. Thousand Oaks, CA: Sage Publications.

———. 2002. *Second Generation: Ethnic Identity Among Asian Americans.* Walnut Creek, CA: Alta Mira Press.

———, and Joann Hong. 2002. Ethnic Attachment Among Second-Generation Korean Americans. In *Second Generation: Ethnic Identity Among Asian Americans,* edited by Pyong Gap Min, 113–28. Walnut Creek, CA: Alta Mira Press.

Moses, Sherri. 1997. Welfare Reform: What Does It Mean for Microentrepreneurs? *Minority Entrepreneur* Jan. / Feb.

Muller, Thomas, and Thomas J. Espenshade. 1985. *The Fourth Wave: California's Newest Immigrants.* Washington, DC: The Urban Institute.

Nee, Victor G., and Brett De Bary Nee. 1972. *Longtime Californ'.* New York: Pantheon Books.

Newman, Katherine. 1988. *Falling from Grace: The Experience of Downward Mobility in the American Middle Class.* New York: The Free Press.

New York Times. 1991. For Immigrants' Children, an Adult Role. Aug. 15.

Nippert-Eng, Christena. 1996. *Home and Work.* Chicago: University of Chicago Press.

O'Dougherty, Maureen. 2002. *Consumption Intensified: The Politics of Middle-Class Daily Life in Brazil.* Durham, NC: Duke University Press.

Ong, Aihwa. 1987. *Spirits of Resistance and Capitalist Discipline.* Albany: State University of New York Press.

———. 1999. *Flexible Citizenship: The Cultural Logics of Transnationality.* Durham, NC: Duke University Press.

———. 2003. *Buddha Is Hiding: Refugees, Citizenship, the New America.* Berkeley: University of California Press.

Ong, Paul, and Suzanna J. Hee. 1994. Economic Diversity. In *The State of Asian Pacific America: Economic Diversity, Issues, and Policies,* edited by Paul Ong, 31–58. Los Angeles: LEAP Asian Pacific American Public Policy Institute and University of California at Los Angeles, Asian American Studies Center.

Osajima, Keith. 1988. Asian Americans as the Model Minority: An Analysis of the Popular Press Image in the 1960s and 1980s. In *Promises and Prospects for Asian American Studies,* edited by Gary Y. Okihiro et al., 165–74. Pullman: Washington State University Press.

Park, John S. W. 2003. Divergent Trajectories: Asian Americans, Latinos, and Contemporary Immigration Law. Paper presented at the Annual Meeting of the Association of Asian American Studies, May 10.

Park, Kyeyoung. 1997. *The Korean American Dream: Immigrants and Small Business in New York City.* Ithaca, NY: Cornell University Press.

Park, Lisa Sun-Hee. 2001. Between Adulthood and Childhood: The Boundary Work of Immigrant Entrepreneurial Children. *Berkeley Journal of Sociology* 45: 114–35.

———. 2002. Asian Immigrant Entrepreneurial Children: Negotiating Work, Family, and Community. In *Intersections and Divergences: Contemporary Asian Pacific American Communities*, edited by Linda Trinh Vo and Rick Bonus. Philadelphia: Temple University Press.

———. 2004. Ensuring Upward Mobility: Obligations of Children of Immigrant Entrepreneurs. In *Asian American Children: A Historical Handbook and Guide*, edited by Benson Tong. Westport, CT: Greenwood Press.

Paules, Greta F. 1993. *Dishing It Out: Power and Resistance Among Waitresses in a New Jersey Restaurant.* Philadelphia: Temple University Press.

Pellow, David N., and Lisa Sun-Hee Park. 2002. *Silicon Valley of Dreams: Immigrant Labor, Environmental Injustice, and the High-Tech Global Economy.* New York: New York University Press.

Perea, Juan. 1997. *Immigrants Out! The New Nativism and the Anti-Immigrant Impulse in the United States.* New York: New York University Press.

Platt, Anthony M. 1969. *The Child Savers: The Invention of Delinquency.* Chicago: University of Chicago Press.

Portes, Alejandro. 1994. Introduction: Immigration and Its Aftermath. *International Migration Review* 28: 632–39.

———. 1997. Immigration Theory for a New Century: Some Problems and Opportunities. *International Migration Review* 31: 799–825.

———, and Min Zhou. 1993. The New Second Generation: Segmented Assimilation and Its Variants Among Post-1965 Immigrant Youth. *The Annals of the American Academy of Political and Social Sciences* 530: 74–96.

———, and Ruben G. Rumbaut. 2001. *Legacies: The Story of the Immigrant Second Generation.* Berkeley: University of California Press.

Prashad, Vijay. 2001. *Everybody Was Kung Fu Fighting: Afro-Asian Connections and the Myth of Cultural Purity.* Boston: Beacon Press.

Pyke, Karen. 2000. "The Normal American Family" as an Interpretive Structure of Family Life Among Grown Children of Korean and Vietnamese Immigrants. *Journal of Marriage and the Family* 62(1): 240–55.

———, and Denise L. Johnson. 2003. Asian American Women and Racialized Femininities: "Doing" Gender Across Cultural Worlds. *Gender and Society* 17: 33–53.

Reed, Adolf, Jr. 2000. *Class Notes: Posing as Politics and Other Thoughts on the American Scene.* New York: The New Press.

Reskin, Barbara, and Irene Padavic. 1994. *Women and Men at Work.* Thousand Oaks, CA: Fine Forge Press.

Rich, Frank. 2003. Had Enough of the Flag Yet? *New York Times*, July 6.

Rohner, Ronald P., and Sandra M. Pettingill. 1985. Perceived Parental Acceptance-Rejection and Parental Control Among Korean Adolescents. *Child Development* 56: 524–28.

Rosenblatt, Roger, ed. 1999. *Consuming Desires*. Washington, DC: Island Press.

Rubin, Beth A. 1996. *Shifts in the Social Contract: Understanding Change in American Society*. Thousand Oaks, CA: Pine Forge Press.

Rubin, Lillian. 1994. *Families on the Fault Line: America's Working Class Speaks About the Family, the Economy, Race, and Ethnicity*. New York: HarperCollins.

Rumbaut, Ruben. 1994. The Crucible Within: Ethnic Identity, Self-Esteem, and Segmented Assimilation Among Children of Immigrants. *International Migration Review* 28: 748–94.

———, and Alejandro Portes. 2001. *Ethnicities: Children of Immigrants in America*. Berkeley: University of California Press.

Saito, Leland T. 2001. The Politics of Adaptation and the "Good Immigrant." In *Asian and Latino Immigrants in a Restructuring Economy*, edited by Marta López-Garza and David R. Diaz, 332–50. Stanford, CA: Stanford University Press.

Sanders, Jimmy M., and Victor Nee. 1996. Immigrant Self-Employment: The Family as Social Capital and the Value of Human Capital. *American Sociological Review* 61: 231–49.

Sarvasy, Wendy. 1997. Social Citizenship from a Feminist Perspective. *Hypatia* 12(4): 54–74.

Sassen, Saskia. 1988. *The Mobility of Labor and Capital: A Study in International Investment and Labor Flows*. New York: Cambridge University Press.

———. 1995. Immigration and Local Labor Markets. In *The Economic Sociology of Immigration: Essays on Networks, Ethnicity, and Entrepreneurship*, edited by Alejandro Portes, 87–127. New York: Russell Sage Foundation.

SBA. *See* U.S. Small Business Administration

Schor, Juliet B. 1991. *The Overworked American: The Unexpected Decline of Leisure*. New York: Basic Books.

———. 1999. What's Wrong with Consumer Society? In *Consuming Desires*, edited by Roger Rosenblatt. Washington, DC: Island Press.

———. 1998. *The Overspent American: Upscaling, Downshifting, and the New Consumer*. New York: Basic Books.

———, and Douglas B. Holt, eds. 2000. *Consumer Society Reader*. New York: The New Press.

Scott, A. O. 2002. You Are What You Drive. *New York Times Magazine*, Sept. 29.

Seattle Times. Times Won't Forget Readers' Reminder on Kwan Headline. 3 / 3 / 2002.

Seelve, Katharine Q. 2004. How to Sell a Candidate to a Porsche-Driving, Leno-Loving Nascar Fan. *New York Times,* Dec. 6.

Siu, Paul C. P. 1987. *The Chinese Laundryman: A Study of Social Isolation.* Edited by John Kuo Wei Tchen. New York: New York University Press.

Song, Miri. 1999. *Helping Out: Children's Labor in Ethnic Businesses.* Philadelphia: Temple University Press.

Strauss, Anselm L. 1987. *Qualitative Analysis for Social Scientists.* New York: Cambridge University Press.

Suarez-Orozco, Carola, and Marcelo M. Suarez-Orozco. 2001. *Children of Immigrants.* Cambridge, MA: Harvard University Press.

Suarez-Orozco, Marcelo M. 1989. *Central American Refugees and U.S. High Schools: A Psychological Study of Motivation and Achievement.* Stanford, CA: Stanford University Press.

Sung, Betty Lee. 1987. *The Adjustment Experience of Chinese Immigrant Children in New York City.* Staten Island, NY: Center for Migration Studies.

Takaki, Ronald. 1989. *Strangers from a Different Shore: A History of Asian Americans.* New York: Penguin Books.

Taylor, Ella. 1989. *Prime-Time Families.* Berkeley: University of California Press.

Thomas, W. I. 1967. *The Unadjusted Girl.* New York: Harper & Row.

Tilly, Charles. 1990. Transplanted Networks. In *Immigration Reconsidered: History, Sociology, and Politics,* edited by Virginia Yan-McLaughlin, 79–95. New York: Oxford University Press.

Tuan, Mia. 1998. *Forever Foreigners or Honorary Whites? The Asian Ethnic Experience Today.* New Brunswick, NJ: Rutgers University Press.

U.S. Department of Commerce. 1997. *Survey of Minority-Owned Business Enterprises: Summary.*

U.S. Small Business Administration, Office of Advocacy. 2001. *Minorities in Business, 2001.* November.

Veblen, Thorstein. 1899. *The Theory of the Leisure Class.* New York: Macmillan Co.

Waters, Mary C. 1999. *Black Identities: West Indian Immigrant Dreams and American Realities.* New York: Russell Sage Foundation.

Weiss, Richard. 1969. *The American Myth of Success: From Horatio Alger to Norman Vincent Peale.* New York: Basic Books.

Wolf, Diane L. 1997. Family Secrets: Transnational Struggles Among Children of Filipino Immigrants. *Sociological Perspectives* 40(3):457–82.

Yoon, In-Jin. 1997. *On My Own: Korean Businesses and Race Relations in America.* Chicago: University of Chicago Press.

Yu, Henry. 2001. *Thinking Orientals: Migration, Contact and Exoticism in Modern America.* New York: Oxford University Press.

Yung, Judy. 1995. *Unbound Feet: A Social History of Chinese Women in San Francisco.* Berkeley: University of California Press.

Yuval-Davis, Nira. 1997. Women, Citizenship, and Difference. *Feminist Review* Autumn (57):4–27.

Zelizer, Viviana A. 1985. *Pricing the Priceless Child: The Changing Social Value of Children.* Princeton, NJ: Princeton University Press.

Zhou, Min. 1992. *Chinatown: The Socioeconomic Potential of an Urban Enclave.* Philadelphia: Temple University Press.

————.1997. Growing Up American: The Challenge Confronting Immigrant Children and Children of Immigrants. *Annual Review of Sociology* 23:63–95.

————, and Carl L. Bankston. 1994. Social Capital and the Adaptation of the Second Generation: The Case of Vietnamese Youth in New Orleans. *International Migration Review* 28:821–43.

————, and Carl L. Bankston. 1998. Growing Up American: How Vietnamese Children Adapt to Life in the United States. New York: Russell Sage Foundation.

Index

Abelmann, Nancy, 15, 16, 139n4
adaptation/assimilation, 1–2, 11–12, 16, 17,
    25, 140nn15,16, 141n43, 144nn12,25,
    145n40; criteria for, 4–5, 112; discipline
    compared to, 24, 26–27, 28, 40–41. *See
    also* social citizenship
adolescents, 65, 148n8; service economy
    employment of, 81; vs. young adults, 18,
    56, 58, 60, 62, 86–88, 125
Adorno, Theodor W., 11–12, 134
affirmative action, 135
African Americans, 143n3; Asian Americans
    compared to, 14, 36; income/class status
    of, 35, 36; self-employment among,
    145n47; self-help ideology among, 132
Alger, Horatio, Jr., 2
American Dream ideology: disciplinary
    nature of, 8, 21; meritocracy, 13, 14, 40;
    rags-to-riches narrative, 2, 15–16, 35,
    88–91, 97; rejection of, 60; role of capi-
    talism in, 7, 62; role of equality in, 5, 8,
    26; role of immigrant family businesses
    in, 3–4, 13–16, 67, 113, 129, 133, 134–36
American family ideology: vs. Asian family
    ideology, 42–44, 49, 63; quality family
    time, 44, 45–47
American Indians. *See* Native Americans
Asian Americans: African Americans com-
    pared to, 14, 36; Asian family ideology,
    42–44, 49, 63; collective identity of, 24,

27–31; income/class status among, 35–36,
    145n42; Latinos compared to, 13, 14; as
    marginalized/the other, 11, 12, 13, 17, 43,
    43–44, 64, 97, 132–33, 136, 140n15,
    141n43, 144n25, 147n1, 148n9, 149n10; as
    model minority, 3, 7, 8, 12, 13, 14, 16,
    23–24, 64, 97, 136, 141n43; Native
    Americans compared to, 14, 36; rates of
    self-employment among, 4, 20, 36–37,
    142n54, 143n80; stereotypes of, 49, 84,
    98–100, 102–5, 107, 118, 149n29. *See also*
    children of Asian immigrant entrepre-
    neurs; immigrant entrepreneurs
Asian immigration, 6, 10, 22–29, 84, 85–110,
    140n28, 141n43, 142n60, 143n3; Chinese
    vs. Korean, 4, 20, 22, 28–31, 36–37,
    142n54, 143n80, 145n40; and homopho-
    bia, 104–5; narratives of children regard-
    ing, 17, 84, 85–110. *See also* immigrant
    entrepreneurs
Asian Indians, 22, 23, 36
Assistance for Families with Dependent
    Children (AFDC), 135

Bankston, Carl, 144n13
belonging. *See* social citizenship
Better Luck Tomorrow, 149n29
Bonacich, Edna, 25, 61–62, 139n4, 144n16
Borjas, George J., 25, 144n16
Bredahl, Carl, Jr., 86

ASIAN AMERICA SERIES

Chinese San Francisco, 1850–1943: A Trans-Pacific Community

YONG CHEN, 2000.

Dreaming of Gold, Dreaming of Home: Transnationalism and Migration Between the United States and South China, 1882–1943

MADELINE Y. HSU, 2000.

Imagining the Nation: Asian American Literature and Cultural Consent

DAVID LEIWEI LI, 1998.

Morning Glory, Evening Shadow: Yamato Ichihashi and His Internment Writings, 1942–1945

EDITED, ANNOTATED, AND WITH A BIOGRAPHICAL ESSAY BY GORDON H. CHANG, 1997.

Dear Miye: Letters Home from Japan, 1939–1946

MARY KIMOTO TOMITA, EDITED, WITH AN INTRODUCTION AND NOTES, BY ROBERT G. LEE, 1995.

Beyond the Killing Fields: Voices of Nine Cambodian Survivors in America

USHA WELARATNA, 1993.

Making and Remaking Asian America

BILL ONG HING, 1993.

Righting a Wrong: Japanese Americans and the Passage of the Civil Liberties Act of 1988

LESLIE T. HATAMIYA, 1993.